WRITING & RHETORIC

Brett C. McInelly & Brian Jackson

HAYDEN
HM
McNEIL

Printed in the United States of America

10 9 8 7 6 5 4 3 2 1

ISBN 978-0-7380-3883-4

Hayden-McNeil Publishing
14903 Pilot Drive
Plymouth, MI 48170
www.hmpublishing.com

McInelly 3883-4 F10 (Writing & Rhetoric)

WRITING & RHETORIC

TABLE OF CONTENTS

Chapter 1

WRITING AND RHETORIC

Getting People on the Same Page

Gregory Clark

INTRODUCTION

In my last year of high school I started hearing stories about "freshman English," stories that turned that class into my biggest worry about starting college. I worried because I knew I would have to take it, and I couldn't find anyone who could tell me what it was. My friends who had taken the course would just roll their eyes and say it was hard. It wasn't until I actually took the class that I found out much more about freshman English. What I found was that it required a lot of reading and a lot more writing, and I had to read very carefully and write very precisely to succeed. And that was hard.

On the first day of class we got our first assignment. The instructor gave each of us a dime, and then asked us to write a paper that described our dime so precisely that he would be able to identify it in a pile of other dimes. On the second day of class we got our second assignment, another paper. This one required us to explain to the instructor what the experience of writing the first paper had taught us about writing. What I had learned, I wrote in the second assignment, is that writing is to be *read* by someone else, someone who needs the information only I can provide. Until then, I hadn't realized that. What I had learned in school about writing had been more about writing than about being read. I had learned how to get words and sentences and paragraphs written down correctly. But the process of describing a dime required me to write to give information to someone else, information that would enable that person to do something he or she needed or wanted to do. I learned that this kind of writing requires me to observe and think carefully in order to choose the right words and phrases, and organize them in the right way, so someone else can understand and *use* the information I give them. What I had learned is that writing is a very practical project, that we write to *communicate*. This is the lesson this course tries to teach.

Almost every college and university in the country requires its first-year students to take this kind of writing course. The writing you do here isn't creative writing, though creativity is certainly involved. The class isn't really a class in grammar, usage, and correct writing, though it teaches these things and you need to learn them. Primarily, this is a class in *writing to communicate with others*. Its purpose is to prepare you to do that successfully in a wide variety of situations where written communication is required. Your college classes put you in many of these situations. In college, writing in one form or another is both the way you learn *and* the way you demonstrate to your instructors and others what you have learned. Thus, one of the first classes you take, or should take, is this first-year writing course.

COMMUNICATION AND COOPERATION

So here we are, in your first-year writing class. Where do we start?

I think we should start where mine did. I don't mean that we should start with the exercise of describing a dime, but with the lesson that exercise taught: writing isn't just about *me*, about what I think or know or observe. Writing is about *us*, about what we are able to know and do together once we get what we think, or think we know, put into words that we each can use. While it really wasn't important that I learned what was unique about my particular dime, it was important that I learned how to notice that uniqueness and then, the hard part, to communicate what was unique about my dime to someone else in order to help that person do what he needed to do—locate my dime in a pile of other dimes. More importantly, my instructor needed to know whether I had learned what he was trying to teach. He needed to evaluate the work and the learning of his students so he could assign us credit and grades. After he read my second paper he knew, at least in my case, that his teaching had succeeded.

The process of writing is part of a larger process of communication. The first-year writing course teaches us how to participate successfully in this process. And we participate in communication by accepting two roles that are, in practice, difficult to separate. We communicate to others things we learn through our study and experience *and*, at the same time, we learn from and use what others communicate to us. We write and we read, we speak and we listen. This is what school and work and the other interactions of life are made of. Successful communication requires us to learn from others and, at almost the same time, enables others to learn from us. Both roles require us to do the work of using words carefully. If you can't get your ideas out of your head to a place where others can access them, and if you have a hard time understanding the ideas of others, you probably won't be very successful.

Communication thus requires the cooperation of different people. Regardless of what you choose to study and what work you choose to do after your studies are complete, your success, both in school and after, depends on your ability to cooperate with others through effective communication. Your success in school requires earning credit and grades and that is really a cooperative process. It requires students to cooperate with teachers by doing the work they are assigned, and it requires teachers to cooperate with students by evaluating that work and acknowledging when it is successful. In school the cooperative process most often occurs through various forms of writing. This is also true in the workplace: success at work occurs when people produce ideas (everything begins with ideas) that others can evaluate and acknowledge as useful, as valuable, as solving their problems and meeting their needs. Most of the time workers document their ideas, whether they are concepts or they are material products, in writing. Again, success requires cooperation and cooperation can't happen without clear and effective communication.

Let's go back to that first college English class of mine. If I had responded to the assignments by studying my dime and then thinking about what the experience taught me about writing but did not write and submit the papers my instructor requested, I would have failed both assignments. Why? I would have failed because my instructor would have had no way to evaluate my work and no way of knowing what I had learned. In school it isn't enough just to learn. We need to communicate what we learn to others in order to make it available for them to use. This is cooperation. For me to do my job—learning—in a way that would allow my teacher to do his—evaluation and certification of my learning—I needed to communicate to him. And I needed to do this in writing to create a record he could keep, review, examine carefully, and respond to specifically. Writing in school can take many forms—a math worksheet or a lab report, a written exam or essay, or even a media-based presentation. But whatever the form, the function is the same. We write in school to learn and, at the same time, to demonstrate and communicate our learning to our instructors.

GETTING ON THE SAME PAGE WITH RHETORIC

Let's sum up what the first-year writing class is about. It is about writing. But it's also a class in communicating, and communicating is about cooperating. In this class, much of that cooperating occurs in the form of careful writing and reading. Basically, what this class teaches is, to use a writing metaphor, how to get yourself and others *onto the same page*.

This ability to get yourself onto the same page with others is fundamental. It is what effective writers and readers do. It is what successful people do. The ability to do this has a name, **rhetoric**, and it is something you can learn.

So what exactly is rhetoric? Is it empty, insincere words? ("Oh, that's just rhetoric.") Is it one-sided statements designed to shut down response? ("I didn't intend for you to answer—that was a rhetorical question.") Is it even more manipulative than that—as in propaganda? ("Hitler's rhetoric mobilized a nation.") Yes. Rhetoric is all of these things we conventionally think it is—and they are mostly negative things. But there is more to rhetoric than most people realize.

Rhetoric is also at work in the good things that communication can do. It is working when honest words tell us the truth in ways that are genuinely helpful. It gets us, together with others, onto the same cooperating page. It is working in statements that invite response, and in responses that improve upon the ideas presented in the initial statements. Rhetoric takes us to the next page together. It is at work when communication changes minds, changes attitudes, and changes actions, hopefully for the better. Those changes take us to new and better pages. Simply put, rhetoric is at work when language does the work of *influence*, when it influences ideas, attitudes, and actions. And, as we all know, influence can work for good or for ill.

So is rhetoric working in the class assignment you write and submit to your instructor? If you are hoping to influence your instructor and, specifically, to influence how he or she will evaluate your work and your learning in the class, you are using rhetoric. Your assignment is rhetorical. Is rhetoric at work when you do good work in your job? It is if you are trying to influence your supervisors and your clients to recognize the value of your services and to reward you positively. Is rhetoric at work when you listen to another person's problems or complaints and then try to advise or to help, or when you try to work out a conflict you have with someone else? It is if you are trying to influence another person to understand things a little differently in order to solve problems or meet goals, if you are trying to get yourself and that person *onto the same page.*

A FEW DEFINITIONS

Think about the idea that rhetoric involves influencing another to think or believe or act cooperatively with you as you read some well-known definitions of the term.

1. Two ancient Greek philosophers, Gorgias and Plato, were suspicious of rhetoric. They were suspicious because they recognized its power. As Gorgias put it, "Words can drug and bewitch the soul" (1948, p. 133). Plato recognized that rhetoric is both unavoidable and necessary, like oxygen, defining it as "a method of influencing men's minds by means of words, whether the words are spoken in a court of law or before some other public body or in private conversation" (1986, p. 73).

2. Another, more practical, Greek, Aristotle, offered a classic definition that is maybe the one most widely acknowledged: rhetoric is "an ability, in each particular case, to see the available means of persuasion" (1991, p. 36). For Aristotle, then, rhetoric is the method of persuading others.

3. A great Roman teacher of rhetoric defined it as "the art of speaking well" (Quintilian, 1856, p. 33). In Rome, by the way, rhetoric was a course of study, in great demand among those who needed to participate in government and in the courts. We might update that definition, given our circumstances, to "the art of speaking and writing well." And "of listening and reading well." Or, probably better, "the art of *communicating* well."

4. A prominent Scottish rhetoric teacher of the eighteenth century, a time when people in Scotland, like people in America, were learning about self-government through processes of debate and discussion, described rhetoric as practical communication—as speech or writing that intends to have particular effects on the persons addressed (Campbell, 2001, p. 902).

5. From the twentieth century we have some definitions of rhetoric that, taken together, are helpful as we try to understand the power of influence. Here are three:
   - Lloyd Bitzer (a communications professor): "Rhetoric is a mode of altering reality, not by direct application of energy to objects, but by the creation of discourse [speech and writing] which changes reality through the mediation of [another's] thought and action" (1968, p. 4).
   - Erika Lindemann (a writing professor): rhetoric "involves more than mere persuasion, narrowly defined.

Discourse that affects an audience, that informs, moves, delights, and teaches, has a rhetorical aim" (2001, p. 40).

- Chaim Perelman (a philosopher): "As soon as a communication tries to influence one or more persons, to orient their thinking, to excite or calm their emotions, to guide their actions, it belongs to the realm of rhetoric" (1977, p. 162).

All of these definitions could be summed up by the definition offered by Kenneth Burke, an American writer, critic, and social theorist (and writing teacher). He said that "Rhetoric is rooted in an essential function of language itself, . . . the use of language as symbolic means of inducing cooperation in [others]" (1969, p. 43). And here we are, back at the principle of cooperation. Whether we are writing and reading, speaking and listening, or even communicating in ways that don't seem to use language at all, we are trying to influence others to cooperate with us, to see the world a little more our way and to recognize that we are trying to see it a little more their way. We do this when we are trying to persuade, when we are trying to inform, even when we are just trying to entertain.

SPEAKING AND LISTENING, WRITING AND READING, AND THE LESSONS OF RHETORIC

As you can see from the definitions I quoted above, people have been thinking and teaching about rhetoric for a long time. It has been a major subject in school since schooling began. Why? Because the study of rhetoric provides a guidebook for communicators and no matter what specialized knowledge or skills we go to school to learn, we are all of us, always, communicating.

When we think about communication we think mostly of the obvious role of the person doing the talking or, for the purposes of this class, the writing. But the role of listener or reader is every bit as important and, in fact, most of us tend to spend more of our time in this role than in the role of writer or speaker. One of the most important lessons of rhetoric is that good communication requires us to take on both of these deeply interwoven roles, and it teaches us how to play both of them well.

An effective writer is also, by definition, an effective reader, since communicating is never a solo act. It always involves a kind of turn-taking process of listening and speaking, reading and writing, of assertion and response.

The elements of this process become clearer if we look more carefully at writing, and understand that it does what spoken communication does and more. Speech happens in the moment. We speak, and then the words are gone except in the memories of those who heard them. But with writing the words remain. When we are in the "listening" role of reader, we can look at those words in a time and place of our choosing, reread them, think about them, even show them to others and get advice before we respond. Writing slows down the exchange of assertion and response that is communication. When we take the time to think about what we have read, to reflect on it, to evaluate it, and to consider things we might say or need to say in response, we are also beginning our turn in the "speaking" role by preparing what we will say or write.

While communication puts us into both of these roles and these roles overlap, they are different in important ways. One requires us to influence and the other to judge an attempt to influence. But they do have as their common ground the work of influence. When we listen we need to be careful, sometimes even wary, of what influence we accept. When we speak we need to be strategic, sometimes even quite assertive, in order to influence others as we want to. Either way we are absorbed in a process of communication, and of cooperation, with others. And if we are to participate in that process well, we need to be thoughtful, careful, and precise in both roles.

Living as we do in the midst of almost constant attempts to influence us (just consider the number of advertisements we encounter each day), our success may be every bit as dependent on the lessons that rhetoric teaches us about being discerning and judicious readers as it is on those that teach us about being clear and persuasive writers. Essentially, we need to understand that every communication situation puts us in a place where someone is trying to influence someone else to believe and even to act in a particular way. If we remember this lesson of rhetoric we will be better prepared to make good choices about what we will accept as well as what we will assert.

PUTTING RHETORIC TO WORK

When people want to get things done with other people, they use rhetoric. When they want others to help them change things, they use rhetoric. We all use it. To some extent, it comes naturally. But successful people have learned how to utilize rhetoric especially well.

Rhetoric began with the study and practice of oratory, of public speaking. When a person speaks in public, and does it well, things can change significantly. This has been true throughout history and it is true today. For most of us oratory is mostly what leaders do in public. Behind closed doors, of course, leaders do a lot of another sort of rhetorical work: negotiation. But in public, much of the job of leadership takes the form of making statements and speeches that attempt to change the ideas and beliefs of an audience. That's what Abraham Lincoln did, and Americans still use the speeches he made about the purpose and principles of the union of the United States to remind themselves of their common purposes and goals. Hitler also used rhetoric to influence the ideas and beliefs of the people he addressed, and people still study his speeches and writings to remind themselves of the frightening power of rhetoric to influence people to agree to do terrible things. And we decide what political leaders to vote into office largely as a result of their public speeches, mostly seen on television and often in the very short form of campaign advertising. We respond positively or negatively to those attempts to influence us and we vote accordingly. And we judge the leaders who are in office not so much on what they do but on how they *explain* what they do when they address us. If they are able to give us explanations with which we feel comfortable, we support them. If they can get us onto the same page with them, we go along—we cooperate.

But there is a lot more rhetoric in our lives than political oratory. There is what you might call commercial rhetoric—the pervasive culture of advertising that saturates our everyday experience. As important as the political attempts to influence us are, the commercial attempts may be more immediately important because they can do us each more immediate good and also more immediate harm. Through the various communication media that surround us—the old forms of print publications, television, radio, and film as well as the new forms of web and pod and wireless communications—we are now immersed in almost constant encounters with influence. Each is an attempt to shape our attitudes and beliefs and desires in order to get our cooperation as consumers. And, on the other side of the communication transaction, many of us will make a living by finding ways to use those media to our advantage. Rhetoric can help us in all of these areas.

Since communication is always an attempt to influence, and the goal of that influence is to gain the cooperation of others in meeting the communicator's needs and reaching his or her goals, a good listener, or reader, recognizes a speaker's goals and responds wisely. A conscientious communicator who is taking a turn at receiving rather than generating the communication must be careful about accepting influence and granting cooperation. Sometimes there is little at stake in this attempt to influence. Sometimes it is just a matter of conveying some facts, of influencing another simply by adding to what that person knows about a situation. But at other times there is a great deal at stake, and the effects of the influence, the consequences of the choice to cooperate, are very important. Rhetoric teaches people how to be wise in making such choices. On the other hand, a communicator who is taking a turn at attempting to influence will need to understand that those being addressed might be wary, even resistant. An understanding of rhetoric might help that communicator find ways to overcome that resistance. When we understand rhetoric we can use it to become more careful, more responsible, about what we read or hear, and more successful in what we write or say.

For a practical example, though, let's leave politics and advertising behind and return to school, to my first-year writing class. Toward the end of the second day of class the instructor handed out a sheet that described the second assignment. It stated exactly what we were to do. Then it offered some brief ideas about what some of those lessons might be and explained the expected length of the paper, some requirements for its form, and its due date. The instructor gave us that assignment sheet after he had finished reading from some of the coin descriptions we had written the day before, trying them out on a pile of dimes on his desk, and commenting quite specifically about their various successes and failures at communicating to him what he needed to know. By the time I got the assignment sheet, I understood from the things he had said in class that what mattered to him was writing that would communicate facts very precisely, and unmistakably, to a particular reader who needed that information for a particular purpose. With that understanding in mind, I read his description of the assignment and realized that, yes, I had learned from the dime assignment that the purpose of writing is to be read and that we write to enable others to know what we know, to understand what we understand, or to do what we can do.

So, I decided, that was how I would answer the question posed by the second assignment. My efforts as a careful reader of the assignment produced an understanding of what I needed to write. I read the assignment sheet carefully and, more importantly, I read my instructor carefully too. I realized what he was trying to teach that day and recognized that the assignment was trying to test whether I had learned it. More importantly, I thought the lesson through and decided it made sense. I decided to accept what he was teaching—his attempt at *influence*—and then I cooperated with him by writing a paper that offered the kind of answer he had hoped the assignment would prompt us to make. I was careful to do this in the form he required and by the due date.

This is the kind of rhetorical situation (see Chapter 3) we find ourselves in most of the time. We read and we learn from reading. As we do so, we decide whether to accept the influence of what we read and then we respond, explaining to someone else what we have learned or what we believe, attempting to influence that person in ways that meet what have become our shared needs. At the end of the process, we're all on the same page.

CONCLUSION

My first-year writing course, like most of them, was as much a course in reading as it was a course in writing. That is because, as we have noted, writing and reading are always entangled: we write in response to reading, our reading prompts our writing, and, of course, writing is always made to be read. However, in this course, as in school, work, and much of the rest of life, it is in writing where, as they say, the rubber meets the road. I could have read my instructor, his assignment sheets, and the course texts more carefully than anyone else and I would not have succeeded in the class, nor learned very much either, unless I did the writing.

We need to also remember the lessons about writing that first-year writing courses teach can apply to ink on the page, words on the screen, and even to recorded spoken words, whether in audio or visual form. And these courses often include these various forms of "writing" in the work they invite students to do. But whatever the form, occasion, or medium, the purpose of all writing remains the same: to influence people, specifically to influence them to share something with the writer, whether a fact, an idea, an understanding, a concern, some conviction, or a plan. The writing can take the form of objective information, of partisan persuasion, or of innocuous (or seemingly so) entertainment. Whatever the form, its function is influence.

The chapters that follow use rhetoric to explain in detail how you can learn to use writing well. Specifically, they explain how to use the kind of writing that is perhaps most important for success in college work, the argument, and then return in some detail to a number of specific principles of rhetoric in order to explain their practical uses for writing in college and beyond. Pay attention and you'll soon be a successful writer, something that involves much more than putting words on a page. It involves getting people onto the same page.

REFERENCES

Aristotle. (1991). *On rhetoric: A theory of civic discourse.* George A. Kennedy (Ed. & Trans.), New York: Oxford University Press.

Bitzer, L. (1968). The rhetorical situation. *Philosophy and Rhetoric, 1,* 1–14.

Burke, K. (1969). *A rhetoric of motives.* Berkeley: University of California Press.

Campbell, G. (2001). *The philosophy of rhetoric.* In P. Bizzell & B. Herzberg (Eds.), *The rhetorical tradition: readings from classical times to the present* (2nd ed., pp. 902–946). Boston: Bedford/St. Martin's.

Gorgias. (1948). *Encomium of Helen.* In K. Freeman (Ed.), *Ancilla to the pre-Socratic philosophers* (pp. 127–138). Cambridge, MA: Harvard University Press.

Lindemann, E. (2001). *A rhetoric for writing teachers* (4th ed). New York: Oxford University Press.

Perelman, C. (1977). *The realm of rhetoric.* Notre Dame: University of Notre Dame Press.

Plato. (1986). *Phaedrus and the seventh and eighth letters.* New York: Penguin Books.

Quintilian. (1856). *Institutes of oratory.* (J. S. Watson Trans.). Retrieved February 23, 2006, from http://www.public.iastate.edu/~honeyl/quintilian/2/chapter15.html

NOTES

NOTES

NOTES

Chapter 2

ANALYSIS OF AN ARGUMENT

What Makes an Argument an Argument?

Grant M. Boswell

INTRODUCTION

If, as Greg Clark observes, rhetoric does the work of influence, then argumentation is a rhetorical genre that attempts to do its work of influence by reasoning. Of course, we often use the word "argument" to describe some kind of verbal altercation. But an argument as we will use the term is not a verbal fight. An argument, for example, is not a fight that you may have had with your parents over what time you were supposed to be home on a school night. Nor is an argument the kind of assertion and denial that may have characterized your "playground" exchanges: "Is so!" "Is not!" An argument is not a zero-sum game in which there is one winner and everyone else loses. Nor is an argument a form of compulsion. There are many things that can do the work of influence, but not all are arguments. Threats, promises, enticements can all influence, but they are not arguments.

An **argument** is a form of persuasion based on reasons. But, as it turns out, there are arguments about what kind of reasoning arguments employ. Some argumentation theorists define arguments from an **analytical point of view**, and some theorists define arguments from a **rhetorical point of view**. So what's the difference and why should it matter to you?

The difference is very important if you are writing arguments, and since that is your task, I want to briefly explain the difference between the analytical approach and the rhetorical approach, so you can understand why the rhetorical approach is more useful for writers of arguments. The difference hinges on how we define reason.

THE ANALYTICAL APPROACH

When Aristotle developed the science of logic, he seemed to be very interested in how one assertion could logically follow from another. When one assertion follows logically from another, it is called a valid inference. Aristotle formalized the **syllogism** as a model of human reason. A syllogism consists of a major premise or assertion, a minor premise or assertion, and a conclusion. Here is an example:

Major premise: All Greeks are mortal.

Minor premise: All Athenians are Greeks

Conclusion: All Athenians are mortal.

This is an example of what Aristotle would call a universal affirmative syllogism because all of the parts are affirmative rather than negative, and each part claims that something is universally true of all Greeks and all Athenians. But, you could negate the claims or you could limit them by claiming, for instance, that "not all Athenians are Greeks." When you count up the possible variations of universal and particular claims, together with affirmative and negative versions, for each of the three propositions of the syllogism, there are 256 possible variations. The problem for Aristotle was determining which of the 256 variations were valid (Fulkerson, 1996, pp. 158–161).

This is the analytical tradition of logical argumentation. It is analytical because it breaks down the syllogism into its parts and examines each possible combination of the parts to see which are valid and which are not. For writers the problem with using reasoning from the analytical tradition is that its primary concern is with validity and not with whether the audience finds the parts persuasive. That is, reasoning is a matter of form and of validity quite apart from the people whom you want to reason with.

THE RHETORICAL TRADITION

For writers there is another, more useful approach to argumentation. This comes through the rhetorical tradition and was also described by Aristotle, although not in the same detail as the syllogism. Quite simply, an argument is one assertion supported by at least one more assertion. This is a very natural form of reasoning that you have been using to your benefit since you were about two. Ever since you learned to use "because" to justify something, you have been making rhetorical arguments. When you told your mother, "I want a cookie," and she asked, "Why?" and you responded, "Because I am hungry," you were making an argument. It is not a particularly good argument, and depending on many factors, it may or may not have been persuasive. What the rhetorical tradition does, however, is take this very natural form of reasoning of one assertion supported by another and make it more likely to be successful when directed at your intended audience.

Let's say I want to argue to an audience that wants to impose greater legal measures on illegal immigration for security reasons, arguing that legal measures probably won't work. How might I go about that? I would want to advance the assertion that "making illegal immigration a felony does not increase the security of our borders" and offer as a supporting assertion that "the threat of a felony charge against people who are willing to die to commit acts of terrorism on our soil does not prevent such people from developing more sophisticated and daring means to enter our country." This is an argument in its most basic form: one assertion supported by another. Of course, the mere statement of the two assertions is not likely to convince my intended audience. I would then need to do some research and elaborate my support by tracing the history of the illegal-immigration problem and its causes, what measures have been successful and which ones haven't been successful, what ingenious measures illegal immigrants have devised in the past, the length of the borders and the difficulty in patrolling them. But an argument that is presented to an audience is merely the elaboration of the two assertions that conceptually make up the argument.

The emphasis in rhetorical argumentation is markedly different from the argumentation in the analytical tradition. The emphasis here is on finding things to say rather than on validity, and on addressing an audience rather than following a formal pattern of inference. In the rhetorical tradition, coming up with something to say about whatever you are going to write or speak about is called **invention** (see Chapter 6). For those of us interested in writing arguments, invention is important. Certainly you have faced the terror of the blank page or computer screen. But more than simply being helpful in coming up with something to say, rhetorical invention must consider the audience in the process. In fact, rhetorical invention derives its substance from the beliefs, values, truths, facts, data, and experts that the audience would accept. Rhetorical argumentation advances the material it invents with attention to language certainly, but also to reasoning with the goal of presenting the best argument possible under the relevant circumstances to the intended audience. Furthermore, rhetorical argumentation makes use of a form of reasoning that you are already familiar with: two assertions joined by "because." As I mentioned, you are so familiar with it that you have been making arguments nearly all your life. We will want to take this form of reasoning and make it serve our purposes, but it is nothing unfamiliar to you or that you can't do fairly easily.

The difference between the two types of argument matters to you as a writer because as you learn to write arguments you are going to be writing them to someone. That is, you will need to consider your audience. Furthermore, rhetorical argumentation relies on a natural form of reasoning rather than on the more formal syllogism. Let's see how this works.

READER RIGHTS AND WRITER OBLIGATIONS

For our purposes as writers of arguments to an audience, we are placing ourselves firmly within the rhetorical tradition of argumentation. And because we are placing ourselves in this tradition of argumentation, we cannot overlook the importance of reasoning with our intended audience. In other words, as writers of arguments we are tied to our readers in very specific ways, and we must acknowledge that readers have rights and that as writers we have obligations to our readers. So what rights do readers have and what obligations do those rights impose on us as writers?

Readers have the right to ask questions they feel an urgent need to have the answer to. Questions that the readers need to have an answer to are called **questions at issue**. Here was a question at issue immediately following the terrorist attacks on September 11: "What is the appropriate response to an act of terrorism on our soil?" Hence, the question of how to respond was at issue.

In addition to some urgency to answer the question, there must also be some indecision about the best way to answer the question. Do we retaliate? Against whom? By what means? Do we act unilaterally or do we form a coalition? Do we follow any procedures before going to war? If so, what are they?

And a question at issue usually has a critical period during which a decision has to be made (see Chapter 3). It has a deadline after which the question at issue begins to lose its urgency. How long do we deliberate before taking action? How long do we give other institutions such as the U.N. a chance to work before we act?

Arguments then arise from questions that are at issue to an audience. The questions at issue are characterized by urgency, disagreement about how to answer the question, and a critical time period. Since we are locating these arguments within the tradition of argumentation that focuses on audience, we can say that arguments arise in situations where the audience has the right to ask questions about the urgency, the means, and the critical time period. In short, the audience has the right to ask, "So what?" In writing arguments, we can never dismiss the audience's right to ask this question. If we write an argument that is persuasive to ourselves but that does not meet the readers' criteria of urgency, means, and time, the audience is left wondering, "So what?"

As we have seen, rhetorical situations develop around questions at issue and the astute writer of arguments will know and prioritize the questions at issue regarding the topic at hand. If this doesn't happen, you are likely to talk past your audience. That is, you may be talking about the same subject matter, say, illegal immigration, but if you are answering one question when your audience is asking another question, you are not likely going to be effective. This problem of talking past one another actually happens very frequently. For practice watch political debates or the political talk shows where a panel of pundits addresses a current topic. You are likely to find that political candidates often don't answer the question asked, but fall back on a prepared position statement, and political pundits talk about the same subject but are really addressing different questions at issue. The result is that the level of public argumentative discourse is not very high, but this does not mean that in the classroom we can't do a much better job. The point is that as writers who want to address our readers, we need to know what is at issue so we do not talk past our audience, and we have to remember that the audience always has the right to ask, "So what?"

RESPONDING TO READERS' RIGHTS

So now we know that readers have rights and that as writers we need to address the readers' right to demand an answer to the issue question. How then do we meet the readers' right to ask, "So what?" We saw above that the question at issue has an element of urgency to the audience.

Many times, the urgency of the questions at issue prompts the question, "What should we do in this case?" For example, if we are concerned that illegal immigration has taken on the new dimension of national security in the wake of September 11, we might ask, "What should we do about illegal immigration in the wake of September 11?" To answer this question we would certainly have to gather some information and do some research along the lines I mentioned above. But there is something else we can do to refine the question.

Questions that we are likely to ask when an issue arises are frequently of the type we noted above: "What should we do in this case?" This type of question is called a **policy question** because it suggests that some kind of policy should result from the answer to the question. Policies, however, always have to be sorted out in terms of what effects they will have. So, before we answer the policy question "What should we do in this case?" we need to ask a question about what effects a proposed policy will have. Underlying all policy questions are questions of effect, or what I prefer to call **questions of consequence**.

When something rises to the level of a question at issue, our first impulse is to ask a policy question. Since September 11, illegal immigration has become bound together with national security. Our first impulse is to ask, "What should we do about illegal immigration now?" There have been many answers to this question. The answers range from building a wall to passing stricter laws against illegal immigration. But to sort out the policies, we now have to push the question at issue down to the level of consequence. Let's take a look at a consequential issue question: What consequence does making illegal immigration a felony have on the security of our borders? All we have done thus far is determine what is at issue for our audience, stated the issue as a policy question (a "should" question), and finally narrowed the question at issue to a question of consequence. We know, however, that if we are addressing an audience on a matter at issue for them, as writers we are obligated to answer the question at issue. How do we go about answering the question of consequence now that we have it?

Remember that we defined an argument as one assertion supported by another. We need to answer the issue question by asserting something. In a question of consequence we always have some kind of policy, proposal, or suggestion being put forward. In this case the proposal is to make illegal immigration a felony. We also have the target or the problem that the audience is concerned about. In this case the proposal of making illegal immigration a felony is aimed at the problem of the security of our borders. So in essence we have two concepts: the proposal and what it is aimed at, or the target. In our example we have the proposal of making illegal immigration a felony, which is aimed at the security of the borders. To meet the readers' right to ask "So what?" we simply need to answer the question by asserting a relationship between the two concepts. By asserting a relationship between the two concepts, I mean we need to supply a verb. We take the first concept "making illegal immigration a felony" and we assert a relationship by supplying the verb "increases" to the second concept—"the security of our borders."

All we have done is to take the concepts of the issue question, the proposal and its target, and answer the question by asserting a relationship between the concepts. In the process we supplied a verb. I will underline the verb to make the parts easy to see. The answer to the issue question looks like this: "Making illegal immigration a felony <u>increases</u> the security of our borders." Now we have an answer to our issue question, but we do not yet have an argument. As we will see, readers have other rights than merely to ask "So what?" But at least we have the beginning of an argument because we have met the readers' right to ask "So what?" and have answered the question at issue. We could just as easily have asserted another relationship between the concepts of our issue question. Maybe something like this: "Making illegal immigration a felony <u>decreases</u> the security of our borders" or "Making illegal immigration a felony <u>does not increase</u> the security of our borders." There are many ways to answer the issue question, but our answer is called the "claim."

THE CLAIM

In asserting a claim, we must make sure that we answer the issue question and that our answer is of interest to our intended audience. In the claims above, we are assuming that the target, the security of our borders, is what our audience is interested in. If it isn't, we have asked the wrong question and we need to return to the issue to ask what question is relevant to our intended audience. Let's say that our audience is interested in sustaining a force of relatively cheap workers to work in fields and factories near the borders. If these people are our intended audience, then secure borders may not be their primary concern. They instead may be concerned about getting people to work for them at wages they can afford to pay and still make a profit. In this case we will have to ask a different issue question with a target that the audience cares about: "What consequence does making illegal immigration a felony have on the labor force for agricultural and industrial employment near the borders?" Now we will have to advance a new claim that answers the issue question and that is directed to our intended audience. We follow the same procedure in revising our claim and supply a verb that asserts a relationship between the proposal and the new target that the audience cares about: "Making illegal immigration a felony jeopardizes the labor force for agricultural and industrial employment near the borders." Answering the issue question provides a claim, but we must make sure that our claim is directed at the interests and values that our readers hold. If the claim is not directed at the values and interests of our audience, we will talk past them and lose the opportunity to make an argument to the people we want to talk to.

So a claim is made by answering the question at issue and by asserting a relationship between concepts in the issue question. This will do for a formal description of the claim, but a better definition is in order. Since we are trying to couch everything we say about argumentation within the rhetorical tradition with its emphasis on audience, it will be better to define a claim in terms of the intended audience. A **claim**, then, is an assertion that answers the question at issue and is initially *unacceptable* to the audience. The unacceptability of the claim is necessary because if the claim were not unacceptable to the audience, there would be no need to make it. And the claim is *initially* unacceptable because after the argument has been made, there is a chance the audience may have been persuaded to hold a belief different from the one it held initially.

MORE READER RIGHTS; MORE WRITER OBLIGATIONS: THE REASON

I mentioned earlier that readers have more rights than merely to ask "So what?" So, you may ask, what other rights do they have? Readers also have the right to ask "Why?" That is, as a writer you are obligated to ask an issue question relevant to your intended audience, answer the question by asserting a relationship between concepts—a relationship that the audience initially finds unacceptable—*and* provide a reason in support of your claim.

I say "a reason" because an argument in its simplest form requires at least one reason, and to advance a simple argument the writer must elaborate all the concepts and relationships entailed in the claim and the reason. Thus, the writer must develop the argument at length, and doing this adequately takes more than simply stating the reason. This will become clearer after we have explained more what is entailed in providing a reason and laying the foundation for the argument, but for now it is important to note that the five paragraph essay structure, with its thesis and three supporting reasons, you may have learned simply won't do to develop a full-fledged argument. But more of this later. Let's return to how we provide a reason.

Just as we did with the claim and the issue question, we need to define the reason in terms of the audience. A **reason** is reasonable, probable, and likely to the intended audience. That is, a reason can be supported. We find support for our reason in all kinds of ways. There are facts, data, and statistics. There are examples and illustrations. There are analogies, principles, comparisons, and contrasts. There are authorities. But the problem with reasons is that they are reasonable, probable, and likely; they usually are not iron-clad, certain, and irrefutable. But neither are they capricious, whimsical, and far-fetched. In order to know when we have good reasons that are reasonable, probable, and likely to our audience, we will invoke the **STAR principle**. STAR is an acronym that stands for **S**ufficient, **T**ypical, **A**ccurate, and **R**elevant (Fulkerson, 1996, pp. 44–53). Let's take each of these up in turn.

SUFFICIENT

The reason must be sufficient. This means that you must have enough facts, data, statistics, examples, illustrations, analogies, principles, authorities, etc. to establish the strength of the reason. A single study may be enough if the study is generally recognized to be the authoritative and definitive study on the matter, but that seldom happens. More often as a writer you have to build your case by accretion, laying layer upon layer of proof until you think you have made the strongest case possible. Sufficient proof, however, is a matter of your judgment as a writer. But if you provide insufficient support, the argument will seem weak and unconvincing. Furthermore, the reader is likely to pass judgment on your ability as a writer and thinker. Your ethos (see Chapter 4) as a writer will suffer, and the reader will form a poor opinion of you and may become increasingly skeptical as the argument proceeds. Even if the rest of the argument is strong, you don't want to create a resistant reader.

TYPICAL

The reason must also be typical. This means that the reasons offered are ones that we would find as being representative of how most informed people understand something or how most experts agree about something or how most research represents something. To explain the seasons in terms of the proximity of the earth to the sun in an elliptical orbit does not meet this criterion because the explanation is not typical among scientists. It is especially important to understand and apply this criterion to your reasons because in this world of Internet research, you can often find studies and data that support all kinds of notions. But providing *any* kind of support is not appropriate; the support must be typical of what reasonable people and experts believe. If you provide evidence from an atypical source, you may be guilty of committing the fallacy of absurdity (*argumentum ad absurdum*). If you provide evidence that most people believe but that is wrong, you are guilty of committing the fallacy of jumping on the bandwagon (*vox populi*). (Fallacies will be discussed in greater detail in Chapter 4.)

ACCURATE

Reasons need to be accurate. In part this means that you as a writer have accurately understood and rendered the information from your sources in a summary, paraphrase, or quotation. In this sense the mark of accuracy is to render something in such a way that the person whom you are summarizing would feel fairly treated. This type of accuracy is especially important if you are summarizing a position that you intend to argue against. If you do not summarize the opposing position accurately, you leave yourself open to a rebuttal, and you again injure the trust you want the reader to have in you. If you skew the summary of an opposing position, you have injured your ethos and have probably made your reader distrust you, and you have committed the fallacy of creating a "straw man." That is, you have set up a straw man that can easily be knocked over.

Accuracy also means that you have found your evidence from the best sources possible. These are reliable sources. They may be first-hand, eyewitness accounts or primary sources. Secondary sources (those that comment on primary sources) are fine, but you must be cautious to use secondary sources that are credible. This usually means that the secondary source has been vetted or has undergone peer review by experts who attest to the legitimacy of the information, methodology, or arguments. These sources include academic books and journal articles. Some sources, such as newspapers or reference works, may certainly be used, but the writer needs to be aware that some newspapers are more credible than others and that some reference works ensure that their entries are written by experts in the fields on which they write. It is always best to corroborate such evidence with other forms of evidence or with more sources than one. Electronic sources are fine so long as they are peer reviewed and credible.

RELEVANT

The reason must be relevant. This seems obvious, but I can't tell you how many times I have written in the margins of student papers, "It may be clear to you what this is doing here, but it isn't to me." In most cases, I don't think the writer is putting in irrelevant information. More likely, the writer has not made it clear to the reader how the information is advancing the argument. Thus, the information is apparently irrelevant. But the writer must remember that the reader does not have the benefit of the research, reading, and mental effort that the author has already put into the topic, so the author must make sure that the criterion of relevance is met. When you summarize, paraphrase, or quote a source, it helps to set it up for the reader by introducing where the information comes from, and afterwards explaining any difficult concepts or words as well as explaining the significance of the information for your purposes. If you fail to make something relevant, you probably have annoyed your reader and have committed the fallacy *non sequitur* ("it does not follow"). Sometimes students are guilty of "padding" their papers by putting in whatever they can find, and, as a result, add irrelevant information.

"BUT WHAT ABOUT . . . ?"

If as a writer you understand that your reason is not irrefutable, but that you want to provide the best possible reasoning that meets the STAR criteria, you are still not assured of having escaped yet another reader right. Readers have the right to ask "So what?" and "Why?" But they also have the right to ask, "But what about this?" That is, as a writer you must assume that you are addressing an intelligent person who won't let you get away with anything and who knows at least as much as you do, if not more. It is, therefore, likely that the reader will have objections or will raise questions. After all, your reasoning is only reasonable, probable, and likely. I call this part of the reason "anticipating the reader's buts" because the reader will probably have several opportunities to ask, "But what about this?" or "But what about that?" The technical name for anticipating your reader's objections is **procatalepsis**. It doesn't matter what you call it, but part of your reason has to involve anticipating your readers' buts, raising the objections in your paper and dealing with them. If you simply avoid the likely objections and go blithely on your way, the reader is likely to raise the objections mentally, and think you are trying to pull a fast one by avoiding them. This again has a damaging effect on your credibility as a writer and makes your reader less willing to trust you and accept the rest of your argument, no matter how careful you have been up to this point.

If you have done the research and read accurate and reliable sources, you have probably come across the claims and counterclaims that you will be dealing with. You will probably have thought them through and have good reasons for believing as you do. Give your reader the benefit of your good reasons. It is a good idea to know the force of the counterarguments. Before drafting your paper, you may want to make the opposing case as best you can in order to know its strengths and weaknesses.

This familiarity with the opposite point of view will help you accurately render that position for your reader, will engender trust in your reader because you are dealing so forthrightly and considerately with the opposing arguments, and will help you make your own case stronger by anticipating the readers' objections. If, however, in the process of making the opposite case, you are persuaded by the evidence that you were wrong or misinformed, you are now in a very good position to argue to people who believed as you once did.

FINDING COMMON GROUND: THE ASSUMPTION

We have seen that an argument arises from a question at issue. A writer answers that question by asserting a claim that the intended audience does not yet agree with and by giving a reason that meets the STAR criteria. But there is one more part to an argument that we need to understand: the assumption. The **assumption** is the underlying logic that links the reason with the claim. The assumption is sometimes stated but more often only implied.

Underlying every simple argument is an assumption, and there are two very important reasons for you to know what the assumption is. First of all it is important for you to know what the assumption is because it is literally the foundation of the argument. The reason and the claim are built upon it. If you have a shaky foundation, the structure is likely to be unstable, so knowing what your assumption is will help insure that you have a solid basis to your argument. But how will you know if your assumption is solid or not? Just as with the other parts of an argument, we need to think about the assumption in terms of the audience.

The second reason why it is important for you to know what your assumption is, is that you need to check it to see if it is something that your audience finds acceptable. The assumption then must be immediately acceptable to your audience. The mark of a good assumption is a response from your audience such as "Of course, what else could it be?" Rarely does the writer ever get the opportunity to pose the assumption to the audience to determine if it is acceptable or not, so the writer has to be able to put him or herself into the shoes of the intended audience to determine whether the assumption is acceptable or not. This is another reason to know both sides to the argument: you begin to have a sense for what your audience thinks and believes. In a class you can test your assumption because every time you say something, one of your classmates may respond with a different point of view. In such a case, you may want to target that student as your intended audience. If you have first-hand acquaintance with someone you believe represents the interests and beliefs of your intended audience, go ahead and pose your assumption to him or her to see the reaction. If you get a shrug of the shoulders and an "Of course, what else could it be?" as a response, you know you have an assumption that will function as common ground. If not, you may have to go back to work on your argument.

We now know that there is an assumption in every argument and that it must be acceptable to our audience, but how do we know what it is, especially if it isn't always explicitly stated? Let's take a look at one of the arguments we began to make when we were first talking about claims: "Making illegal immigration a felony <u>decreases</u> the security of our borders." In order to complete the argument we need to add a reason to the claim.

> Making illegal immigration a felony <u>decreases</u> the security of our borders because, as long as the U.S. economy creates the "pull effect," the potential deterrence of the felony charge <u>will encourage</u> illegal immigrants to develop more sophisticated and daring means to enter our country.

Here is one possible argument. So where is the assumption? I have underlined the verbs in order to show you where the assumption is. I also need to number the verbs to keep track of which verb we are talking about. The verb in the claim is verb #1. The verb in the reason is verb #2. The assumption is implicit, meaning that the assumption is literally "folded in." To unfold it we need to know which verb is in the claim and which is in the reason. To make the assumption explicit all we need to do is plug the parts of our argument into this formula:

"*Whatever* Verb #2 + the rest of the reason *also* Verb #1 + the rest of the claim." In the argument above the assumption is this:

> *Whatever* <u>will encourage</u> illegal immigrants to develop more sophisticated and daring means to enter our country *also* <u>decreases</u> the security of our borders.

The assumption in this case is something that most people would agree with; that is, there is a logical relation between the reason and the claim.

CONCLUSION

An argument is actually a fairly simple conceptual structure, but it is essential that we know what its parts are and how each part relates to our audience. Without knowing the parts and how they relate to our readers, we cannot make effective arguments.

But one matter that we haven't dealt with yet is why we bother making arguments. We must acknowledge that not all arguments are successful. You may do all the work I have described above and write what you think is the best possible argument in support of a specific claim and still leave your reader unconvinced. Was it worth doing? I would have to answer, "Yes, it was." Why make arguments if all arguments can simply be met with other arguments, none of which is irrefutable and convincing once and for all? The answer is that the alternative is unthinkable or unbearable. If arguments relied on compulsion, there would be no such thing as choice. No choice, no possibility of freedom. If choices were made solely on the basis of whim or caprice, there would be no order or predictability in human affairs. Between compulsion and capriciousness is the work of argument, and most of the institutions that we as humans value depend on argument. Can you imagine a justice system or a political system based on compulsion or whim? Such institutions would render neither justice nor good government. Yes, we must admit that sometimes in the justice and political systems we make mistakes, but can you think of a better way of proceeding? Think of all the ways that we as humans make decisions and policies. Are force or caprice preferred to what we have, imperfect though it be, in which we attempt to make arguments to determine how and what we do? In the words of Chaim Perelman and Lucie Olbrechts-Tyteca (1971), authors of perhaps the most important treatise on argumentation in the twentieth century,

> Only the existence of argumentation that is neither compelling nor arbitrary can give meaning to human freedom, a state in which a reasonable choice can be exercised. If freedom was no more than necessary adherence to a previously given natural order, it would exclude all possibility of choice; and if the exercise of freedom were not based on reasons, every choice would be irrational and would be reduced to an arbitrary decision operating in an intellectual void. (p. 514)

I think it's worth it; I hope you do too.

REFERENCES

Fulkerson, R. (1996). *Teaching the argument in writing.* Urbana, IL: NCTE.

Perelman, C. & Olbrechts-Tyteca, L. (1971). *The new rhetoric: A treatise on argumentation.* (Trans. J. Wilkinson & P. Weaver). Notre Dame, IL: University of Notre Dame Press.

NOTES

NOTES

NOTES

Chapter

KAIROS AND RHETORICAL SITUATION

Gary Layne Hatch

INTRODUCTION

Students often study arguments apart from any social context. They are often presented with a collection of written arguments lined up like zoo animals removed from their native habitat. Consequently, many students fail to realize that arguments are all around them. They may fail to realize that arguments make up an important part of how they live, work, and study every day. Whenever we are engaged with ideas and reasons, we are arguing. Whenever someone else makes a claim on our opinions, beliefs, and values, we are arguing. But placing arguments in context includes more than simply identifying who is engaged in arguing—the speakers and listeners, or writers and readers. The context for arguing also includes the time, places, and circumstances (Bitzer, 1968). When you understand the complete context for an argument, you will be better able to make sense of the argument and respond effectively.

Writing that matters, including argumentative writing, responds to the needs of actual people in real situations. When you argue, you are part of a conversation made up of the members of a community who care about the issue you are discussing. Others may respond to your argument, inviting you in turn to reply to their response. This interaction between writers and readers is called a **rhetorical situation**. A rhetorical situation is defined by the elements in any act of communicating: the writer/speaker, the audience (reader/listener), the purpose, the subject or issue, and the occasion. Figure 1 shows the primary parts of the rhetorical situation: the writer, the reader, and the issue.

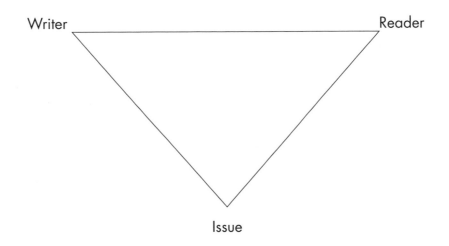

Figure 1

This interaction is mediated through symbols—language, of course, but visual symbols too. If you are in the position of the "writer," then you are making an argument through language or visual elements that addresses the issue under discussion. If you are the "reader," then you are trying to understand someone else's argument. In reality, we often take turns being the writer/speaker or the reader/listener.

A rhetorical situation is one that calls for the use of persuasion—it's a situation in which an argument would be an appropriate response. It's a significant moment that calls for a rhetorical response. Of course, because arguments are everywhere, rhetorical situations are everywhere too. Whenever true arguing occurs, it happens within the context of a rhetorical situation. Regardless of the reading or writing task, determining the rhetorical situation is key to understanding your role as a reader or writer. Understanding the rhetorical situation will help you define your purpose, audience, and subject much more clearly. And identifying your position in the rhetorical situation is essential to arguing effectively.

KAIROS AND KRONOS: TWO CONCEPTS OF TIME

Time is an essential element of rhetorical situations. Indeed, you could define the art of rhetoric as the art of knowing how to say the right thing to the right people at the right time. But what is the *right* time? The ancient Greeks had two concepts of time: *kronos* and *kairos*. **Kronos** is our typical concept of time, something that passes at a regular rate, measured in seconds, minutes, hours, or days. The word *kronos* persists in our English words *chronology* (the study of the passage of time) or *chronometer* (a device for measuring time—a fancy word for "clock"). To understand this kind of time, imagine a line extending to infinity in both directions (see Figure 2). The center of the line is the "present" and the arrows pointing in both directions represent the past and the future. This represents *kronos*.

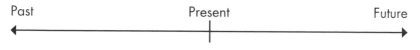

Past   Present   Future

Figure 2

Kairos presents a different concept of time, a concept based on the significance of the moment: it is "the opportune moment" or proper time to act. The Hebrew author of Ecclesiastes expresses this view of time in this famous passage:

> To every thing there is a season, and a time to every purpose under heaven. A time to be born, and a time to die; a time to plant, and a time to pluck up that which is planted; a time to kill, and a time to heal; a time to break down, and a time to build up; a time to weep, and a time to laugh; a time to mourn, and a time to dance; a time to cast away stones, and a time to gather stones together; a time to embrace, and a time to refrain from embracing; a time to get, and a time to lose; a time to keep, and a time to cast away; a time to rend, and a time to sew; a time to keep silence, and a time to speak; a time to love, and a time to hate; a time of war, and a time of peace. (KJV 3:1–8)

Some moments in time are fraught with significance. Other moments in time pass without much notice. Just as time seems to move at a different rate when our attention is engaged ("time flies when you're having fun"), so some moments are more memorable than others because of their significance to us. One generation of Americans can remember where they were and what they were doing when they heard that President John F. Kennedy had been shot. Another generation remembers vividly watching the space shuttle Challenger explode on live television. Most Americans remember the morning of September 11, 2001. People remember the day they were married, the birth of a child, the death of a friend or family member, their graduation from high school or their first day on a new job. Unlike other days, these moments were full of significance, and as a result, these moments stand out in the flow of time. They are moments of *kairos* in the flow of *kronos*.

THE RIGHT PEOPLE UNDER THE RIGHT CIRCUMSTANCES

As may be evident from the examples I just provided, *kairos* is really about more than just the right time. *Kairos* refers to any moment that is somehow a critical juncture of time, space, and action. It's the right people at the right place at the right time and under the right circumstances. These critical moments can take different forms. They may be regular meetings, such as town council meetings, court sessions, public hearings, stockholders' meetings, church meetings or committee meetings. These may be ceremonies or rituals, such as weddings, funerals, graduations, or birthdays. One kind of action that critical moments such as these can call forth is communication. For example, guests at a wedding may toast the newlyweds. Graduation ceremonies and funerals have speakers. Proclaiming a new national monument, winning or losing an election, announcing a new tax plan all require a suitable rhetoric—saying the right thing to the right people under the right circumstances.

A rhetorical situation brings members of a community together to discuss a particular issue, but the issue and the relationships among the participants in the conversation make sense only if you can identify the community or communities that these participants belong to. The word *community* comes from the Latin word *communis,* which means "shared" or "common." In its broadest sense, *community* describes a group of people who have something in common. Communities may be defined by geographical location or may consist of people who have a shared history, language, or culture. Communities may be formed by those who share the same social or business interests or the same political or religious views. Academic disciplines, departments in a college or university, and scholarly organizations often define themselves according to a common body of knowledge or domain of study, or shared methods of inquiry.

Communities overlap and intersect in a lot of interesting ways. Communities formed by shared interests or beliefs may transcend geographical boundaries, and a geographical community may contain many smaller communities defined by a common language or culture. And people may claim membership in a lot of different communities. For example, members of your class (one community) may belong to a variety of other communities according to where they come from, where they currently live, where they attend church, what social events they participate in, what campus clubs they have joined, or who they associate with. Even though you and your classmates form one type of community (your class), you would no doubt interact with each other in a different way in a different community— if, for example, you met at a sporting event or a political rally. We all belong to different communities, but we also share our membership in communities with others. Identifying ourselves with our different communities gives us our diversity, but because this membership is based on commonalities and shared beliefs and values, membership in communities also unites us.

DISCOURSE COMMUNITIES

One element of community that unites us is language. Nearly all people who interact with one another in a community do so through a common language. This common language helps to define any community because language initiates us into the world of a community and allows us to participate through the power of communication. (Notice that the word *communication* has the same Latin root as *community.* By its nature, language allows us to "share.") As members of a community, we learn the common names for people, places, objects, actions, and emotions. Through the language of the community, we receive the community's common values and beliefs. Another name for this shared language is "discourse," and a community defined by language is often called a **discourse community**.

A university or college is a discourse community. The boundaries of the college community are not only defined by the geographic space and physical barriers of the campus but also by language. Terms from the college discourse community include, among many others, "associate professor," "credit hour," "add/drop," "general education," "syllabus," "final exam," and "quad." Some first-time college students struggle with this language, and this struggle is part of what identifies them as newcomers to more experienced members of the community. Often no one bothers to define these terms for newcomers because more experienced members of the community have forgotten that there was a time when the terms weren't familiar. The problem of learning the discourse of the college community is compounded by the fact that the larger university is made up of many smaller discourse communities defined by separate disciplines, departments, majors, and fields of study. For example, the discourse of the humanities is quite different from the discourse of the social sciences or physical and biological sciences. If you study art history, for instance, you learn the names of the formal elements of art, the names of significant artistic movements, key figures in the history of art, and ways of interpreting and evaluating art. You would also learn ways of understanding art works within their own time period as well as examining the significance of the work within our own time. If you studied evolutionary biology, however, you would learn a very different discourse, the language of theoretical and experimental sciences, closely tied to the language of mathematics.

The campus community also overlaps with other communities defined by a diversity of cultures, religions, political views, and shared interests. Students on a typical college campus come from all over the United States and many parts of the world. They bring with them a unique mix of the communities that they identify with. Understanding that you are part of these various communities is important to help you know who the "right people" are to address in a particular rhetorical situation. Who you need to talk to depends on the shared language, beliefs, and values that define the community you belong to.

THE ORGANIZATION OF COMMUNITIES

Every community has a structure, an organization of power, a hierarchy of positions and roles taken by individuals within the community. The structure of the community can be fairly simple, or very complex, as with a government body or corporation, which may have organizations within organizations. There may be a formal, recognized structure as well as an "unofficial" structure behind the official one, a "shadow" organization. Considerable power, for example, may lie in the hands of staff or support people who work behind the scenes.

The university or college community that you belong to as a student is a complex organization, an organization made up of many smaller organizations. The structures of these organizations may overlap, often in confusing ways. Beginning students are often frustrated because they don't understand who to go to for help with a problem, who has the power to make and enforce decisions, or who they can talk to when they have questions. For example, what would you do if you became ill during finals week and couldn't take your exams? Most colleges have a well-established system for dealing with just such emergencies. You could usually contact your teachers or talk to someone in the departments that offer the courses you are taking. You could then request an "incomplete," a grade that allows you to complete the work for the course at a later time. But even though this procedure is well known to faculty and administrators at the university, it probably isn't well known to students. How would students know about such a policy? It's usually contained in the policies section of a university catalog, but few students read this from cover to cover. But to be successful as a student, you need to learn how the system works.

Understanding the structure of the community—its distribution of power, its processes for communication and decision making—is an essential part of living in any community. Persuasive power can come from knowing how to say something that matters to the people that matter. But who are these people? And how can you get access to them?

For questions of public policy, the people who matter are those who have the power to make a change. These are the decision makers. Not everyone in a particular community has equal power or access to the political process. For example, you can debate an important social issue with your friends around the lunch table, but this debate probably won't have as much of an impact on the life of the community as it would if you could somehow present your views to a member of Congress, a lobbyist, or an influential member of the media. Although you can contact your Congressional representative, you probably wouldn't have the same influence as someone who can visit the representative face to face or hire an expensive team of lobbyists.

People who matter are also those who can give you access to conversations in the community, those who can help you to make your voice heard. Lawyers, for example, have greater access to the courts than do ordinary citizens. Newspapers and magazines have editors and publishers who decide which voices are heard in these publications. Television and radio stations have managers who decide what gets on the air. Even radio call-in programs, which appear to be very democratic, have a producer who decides which callers get on the air. Scarcity of time, space, and money limits the number of people who can join the conversation and how much they can contribute. Those who control access to the conversation are called "gatekeepers." To make a real difference, you need to know the process by which gatekeepers will allow access to meaningful conversations, and you will need to influence or gain the attention of these gatekeepers.

But just because you're not a decision maker or a gatekeeper doesn't mean you don't have influence. Understanding something about arguing, the organization of communities, and the nature of rhetorical situations may allow individuals greater access to power than they realize is possible. Sometimes a few letters to a member of Congress can influence his or her vote on an issue, particularly when the issue is not a highly publicized one. And although your influence may be small on national issues, you can wield considerable influence in your family, within your circle of friends, on your campus, or in your local community. The power of language also provides individuals with the power to organize, and in matters of public policy, there often truly is strength in numbers.

WHAT ARE THE RIGHT CIRCUMSTANCES?

Influencing people who can make a difference is not enough by itself. You have to address them under the right circumstances. For example, getting the right people in the right place is crucial. Discussions about issues important to a community take place in church buildings, courtrooms, boardrooms, student unions, and town halls. Nearly every university has a place on campus that is considered the "right place" to speak out on public issues (either by tradition or administrative decree). For example, at the University of Utah, there is a big rock near the Olpin Student Union that is defined as a "free-speech zone." At Arizona State University, people gather near the fountain in front of the student union or the lawn west of the library. Here they discuss politics and religion but also promote campus and club events. At Brigham Young University, students generally meet at "Brigham's Square," just outside the Wilkinson Student Center, where the university's student association occasionally sponsors a "soap box," an open microphone for students to speak out on issues of local concern. Colleges also have more formal spaces for discussion, such as classrooms, seminar rooms, or auditoriums. These have a different set of rules from, say, the fountain in front of the student union.

Time is also a consideration. Some occasions for arguing arise out of a particular crisis or moment of decision, but others are regularly scheduled in a community. City councils, courts, stockholders' meetings, and government hearings, for example, all follow a regular schedule for conducting their business. If you want to argue a local issue in front of the city council, you need to know both the place and time of the meeting and the process for getting your issue on the agenda.

Circumstances do make a difference. If you met the nine members of the Supreme Court at a party in Washington, D.C. and asked each his or her opinion on the landmark abortion-rights case *Roe v. Wade*, you wouldn't get an official Supreme Court opinion because although you have the right people, you would have them in the wrong place and at the wrong time.

THE LIFE CYCLE OF RHETORICAL SITUATIONS

To argue effectively, you need to know how to craft a suitable response to the right people under the right circumstances. Knowing how to do this requires that you know something about how rhetorical situations change over time. Such situations are not static; they evolve. How you respond to the situation depends on where it is in this process of development. Lloyd Bitzer, an important rhetorical theorist, calls the evolution of a rhetorical situation its "life cycle" (as cited in Hauser, 2002, p. 38).

In the earliest stages of this cycle, a need for debate exists, but the circumstances may not be clearly defined. Some people may not be aware of the issue or may not have organized themselves to respond to it. At this point, arguing can define the issue more clearly and raise awareness of the problem. As the situation evolves, it reaches a period of maturity where people are forming their opinions, arguing their positions, and beginning to make decisions. This time of maturity is *kairos*, the crucial moment to respond to the right people under the right circumstances. As this critical moment begins to pass, Bitzer explains that rhetorical situations enter a period of deterioration. At this stage, many people may already have formed their opinions, made their decisions, or begun to take action or implement plans. As people's opinions harden, it grows increasingly difficult for arguing to have an effect. Finally, the rhetorical situation enters a period of disintegration in which arguing can have little or no effect. Perhaps those who can make a difference have already made their decision or turned their attention to other matters. Perhaps plans are already completed or well under way (Hauser, 2002, pp. 38–40).

THE LIFE CYCLE OF A RHETORICAL SITUATION

Origin: The awareness of the issue is still forming, and the implications are unclear. Many people are unfamiliar with the issue or may not have strongly held opinions. The processes for discussing or deciding the issue are largely undetermined. Few groups may be involved in the process.

Maturity: The issues are more clearly defined, and processes for discussing and deciding the issue are in place. The moment of decision is approaching. Many different groups are engaged in the decision-making process. This is the critical moment (*kairos*).

Deterioration: The prime moment for influencing the opinion of decision makers has passed, and a solution may be in the early stages of implementation. Positions on the issues are well established.

Disintegration: The process of change becomes practically irreversible. Decisions have been made and put into action. Many groups have moved on to other issues.

Here is an example of the life cycle of a rhetorical situation. The state of Utah is considering building a freeway that would pass through wetlands near the shores of the Great Salt Lake. Proponents of this freeway believe it is needed to handle current levels of traffic as well as anticipated growth. Many environmentalists and some local residents fear that the freeway will destroy hundreds of acres of vital wetlands. In the early stages of this project, opponents of the freeway try to raise public awareness of the issue and of the importance of the wetlands and try to shape the process by which this issue will be discussed and decided. The primary approach here is to get the attention of the media gatekeepers and get the environmentalists' views on the public agenda. Once the process for discussing and deciding the issue is defined, the rhetorical situation reaches a point of maturity. All parties put forth their best arguments to the decision makers at the scheduled times and places. In this case, the state decides to hold a series of local hearings before debating the issue in legislative committee and making a decision. Those opposed to the freeway continue to raise public awareness and to persuade people to attend the hearings and make their voices heard (as do those who favor the freeway). When the process reaches the legislative stage, the environmental group works through lobbyists and tries to organize a letter-writing campaign for those legislators who are on the committee or who have influence on this issue. Once these hearings end and the committee makes its recommendation, the situation enters a period of deterioration. It becomes harder and harder to influence legislators and shape public opinion. After the vote is taken and the process of building the freeway begins, the rhetorical situation disintegrates, and the environmental group has to move to a new rhetorical situation, trying to get a court injunction against building the freeway.

DECORUM: A SUITABLE RESPONSE

Significant moments in time often require a fitting response. Special occasions may require that we dress or act in a certain way. A wedding dress, a graduation cap and gown, a Halloween costume, a judge's black robes, a soldier's dress uniform: all of these different ways of dressing indicate a recognition of what is appropriate or fitting for a particular occasion. Even when we go to a party or a dance, we dress a certain way, recognizing that these occasions are different from other occasions and require a different response. Acting in a way that is inappropriate for the situation shows a lack of decorum, for as one ancient Greek writer observes, "everything done at the right time is seemly and everything done at the wrong time is disgraceful" (as cited in Sprague, 2001, p. 283).

When you adapt your argument to the needs of an audience, you need to be careful to follow the conventions that guide the particular conversation you are joining. Each discourse community has its own rules governing what is "sayable," about what is understandable or acceptable. Generally, the more you conform to a community's conventions the more credibility you have with that community and the more persuasive you will be. You'll notice, for example, that when a political candidate addresses a particular group, he or she adapts to some of the conventions of that group. When addressing a group of college students, a candidate will usually dress down and try to identify with a younger crowd. As a candidate, Bill Clinton demonstrated this when he did his famous interview with MTV in 1994. He wore sunglasses and played the saxophone and answered questions about what kind of underwear he prefers (boxers or briefs?). When addressing a group of bankers, a candidate would dress in a suit and talk finance. When George W. Bush delivered his famous speech declaring the end to major combat operations in Iraq (the "mission accomplished" speech), he flew onto an aircraft carrier and emerged from the navy jet dressed in a pilot's jumpsuit. There isn't a guidebook to tell candidates how to dress and act when speaking before a particular group, but a successful candidate will find a way to "speak their language."

When you observe the workings of a community, pay attention not only to what people say, but also to how they say it. Saying the right thing in the right way is an art, and typically those who wield the most influence in a community have mastered it. You can develop your own sense of decorum by imitating those who are successful and finding a way to make their strategies your own.

DEFYING DECORUM

Although the best way to persuade others is to identify with them in some way, still there are some who are successful by doing just the opposite. Refusing to follow the conventions of a community, particularly if done in a dramatic way, can get the conversation going, redirect a conversation, or draw attention to an issue that might otherwise go unnoticed.

Those who challenge the community cause us to see the familiar in unfamiliar ways. They make the ordinary seem strange and new. They cause us to think about things that we would otherwise take for granted. We go through much of our lives without thinking much about what we do. Our experience becomes habitual and automatic. Think about some things you do every day—driving the car, taking a shower, getting dressed, eating breakfast. You have probably developed some routines that have become so mechanical that you don't even have to think about what you're doing. We also tend to follow routines in our habitual ways of thinking. Such routines are efficient, but by following them, we can develop blind spots. Someone once observed that we have become like fish in a fish bowl: we don't notice the water because it surrounds us. Artists, philosophers, and writers may challenge our ways of seeing, thinking, and perceiving the world. Andy Warhol was able to draw our attention to something as ordinary as Campbell's soup cans by framing them as art, challenging our conventional beliefs about what counts as "art." Socrates challenged the conventional thinking of fifth-century Athens by asking questions, exposing those who made false claims to wisdom. Abraham Lincoln credited Harriet Beecher Stowe with starting the Civil War because of the way *Uncle Tom's Cabin* caused a nation to reconsider its attitudes toward slavery. Martin Luther King, Jr. changed how many people saw the Civil Rights Movement through his "Letter from Birmingham Jail." Political activists and protestors may defy traditional decorum in order to draw attention to an issue that might otherwise go unnoticed.

Those who defy decorum do so at great personal risk. Not all members of a community will welcome the challenge and may threaten or alienate those who do things differently. But those who challenge the traditions of the community can play an important role in maintaining its vitality by helping us out of the mental ruts we can fall into through habitual ways of thinking.

CONCLUSION: TAKING ACTION

Novelist Ernest Hemingway warned us, "Never mistake motion for action" (Cole, n.d., para. 2). As the rhetorical theorist Kenneth Burke explains, action is motion with a purpose (Burke, 1945, p. 14). If you trip and fall down the stairs, you are moving but not acting. For many people, life is motion rather than action. Things happen to them that seem beyond their control. They are caught up in the flow of time (*kronos*) and seem to be victims of circumstance. Of course, we can never entirely escape our circumstances, but those who understand the power of language to shape and respond to significant moments in time (*kairos*) can gain some power over their circumstances and expand their individual freedom and influence. They become agents—those who can act—rather than those who are acted upon. The key to being able to influence the world around you is being able to see the rhetorical nature of these situations, the interactions among writers, readers, issues, and circumstances. By doing this, you can learn to craft a fitting response to these situations.

REFERENCES

Bitzer, L. (1968). The rhetorical situation. *Philosophy and Rhetoric, 1,* 1–14.

Burke, K. (1945). *A grammar of motives.* Berkeley: University of California Press.

Cole, M. (n.d.). *Cole's quotables.* Retrieved June 5, 2006, from http://www.quotationspage.com/quote/3793.html

Hauser, G. (2002). *Introduction to rhetorical theory.* Long Grove, IL: Waveland.

Sprague, R. (2001). *The older sophists.* Indianapolis, IN: Hackett Publishing.

NOTES

NOTES

NOTES

Chapter

RHETORICAL PROOFS

Ethos, Pathos, and Logos

Gary Layne Hatch

INTRODUCTION

In his famous definition of rhetoric (included among those presented in Chapter 1), Aristotle (1991) defines rhetoric as "an ability, in each particular case, to see the available means of persuasion" (p. 36). Let's take a closer look at this definition. The Greek word that Aristotle uses for "ability" is *dynamis,* which means "ability, capacity, or faculty." This Greek word should be familiar as the root of such English words as *dynamic, dynamo,* or *dynamite.* What do these words all suggest? Something that is active, forceful, and powerful. So rhetoric is the *power* to be able to see, for any particular rhetorical situation, all of the possible ways of persuading someone. Thus, rhetoric can be seen as the art of discovering possibilities. Which of these possibilities you choose depends on your particular rhetorical situation.

The Greek word that Aristotle uses to describe "means of persuasion" is *pisteis,* a word often translated as "proof," but this word also means "conviction, belief, trust, evidence, or assurance." This Greek word is the word used in the New Testament for "faith." So the "means of persuasion" or *pisteis* are the ways in which you build your audience's trust or faith in your message. What Aristotle describes are strategies that a speaker or writer could use to instill belief in others. This is particularly important in a situation where there isn't necessarily an absolute truth, where there is uncertainty or controversy. What strategies are likely to cause people to think more about a message to the point that they may actually change how they think about it? Aristotle describes three proofs: persuasion through a writer's credibility (**ethos**), persuasion through a reader's emotions (**pathos**), and persuasion through reasoning (**logos**).

ETHOS: ESTABLISHING CREDIBILITY

According to Aristotle, we are more likely to believe someone who is good. In fact, Aristotle calls one's character "the controlling factor in persuasion" (1991, p. 38). He uses the Greek word *ethos* to describe a persuasive strategy built on trust. This Greek word should be familiar as the root of the word *ethics*.

Think about people you trust. Why do you trust them? You might trust them because they have authority. For example, they may hold a certain position in the community. Religious leaders, teachers, police officers, and other public officials have authority because of the position they hold. The uniform, the badge, the sign of office are all persuasive in some contexts. Their authority can make them more credible. For instance, the President of the United States has certain authority because of his position—he can put ideas into action—and the office he holds conveys a certain degree of credibility on whomever holds the position. In the movie *The American President*, fictional president Andrew Shepherd describes the White House as "the single greatest home-court advantage in the modern world."

Others gain our trust, not because of the position they hold, but rather because of the qualities of character they demonstrate. Generally, we trust people who are knowledgeable and experienced, who are decent, fair, reliable, and honorable, and who demonstrate goodwill with others. We tend to trust people who are more like us, who identify with our values and beliefs. You might also trust someone because of his or her knowledge of an issue. Because we can't know everything about every issue we need to form an opinion on, we often value the opinion of experts. For instance, most people want to find a good doctor or dentist, one who is not only knowledgeable and skilled, but also honest and caring.

In a classic experiment conducted in 1951, social psychologists Carl Hovland and Walter Weiss did an experiment that showed the influence of credibility on persuasiveness. They gave two different groups of people the exact same written message arguing for the feasibility of building nuclear-powered submarines. One group was told that the argument was written by J. Robert Oppenheimer, a famous atomic physicist who had worked on the Manhattan Project (the project that developed the first atomic bomb). The second group was told that the argument was translated from *Pravda*, the official newspaper of the Soviet Communist party, widely regarded as a propaganda outlet for the Soviet Union. A large number of those who believed that the argument came from Oppenheimer changed their opinion, but very few did who believed that the argument came from *Pravda* (Aronson, 1999, p. 75). Similar experiments have shown what most of us would take to be obvious: "that a judge of a juvenile court is better than most people at swaying opinion about juvenile delinquency, that a famous poet and critic can sway opinion about the merits of a poem, and that a medical journal can sway opinion about whether or not antihistamines should be dispensed without a prescription" (Aronson, 1999, p. 75). What makes the difference here? Someone who is credible is seen as good, knowledgeable, and reliable.

Within the Catholic community, the Pope has credibility because of his position, and his credibility is enhanced by his well-known acts of service and devotion, his theological writings, and his years of experience in church leadership. When the Pope speaks or writes on religious issues, he can rely heavily on his position and reputation. Supreme Court justices also have considerable credibility by virtue of their position, education, and experience. Even though other members of the legal community may know as much as or even more than a Supreme Court justice about particular legal issues, a Supreme Court justice has considerable influence by virtue of having been appointed to the court.

But even those who hold positions of responsibility and influence need to rely to a certain degree on the art of rhetoric to be persuasive. Those who are relatively unknown must rely on these arts even more. For instance, because of their traditional role in the academic community, students are typically in a position where they may have limited credibility.

Consider, for example, the traditional research paper. Teachers expect students to include their own reflections and conclusions, but teachers also expect students to rely heavily on the opinions of experts and authorities. Students quote, paraphrase and summarize other writers, merging their voices with voices of authority to create credibility and show what they have learned about their topic. If a research paper came in with very few references, the teacher would probably be suspicious, perhaps wondering whether the student was guilty of plagiarism.

Teachers have different expectations for their fellow teachers and scholars. In an essay by an established scholar, a lot may be left unsaid because there is a body of common knowledge and assumptions about the topic that one has mastered as an expert. Established scholars rely much more upon their own authoritative voices and less upon the voices of others. Saying something that everyone else knows can label one as a beginner. Of course, experienced scholars still cite their sources, but the kind of sources they cite and the way in which they talk about their subject demonstrates that they are knowledgeable. For students to achieve this same kind of credibility, they also need to learn to talk about their subjects in a knowledgeable way. When a student opens an essay with a sweeping, panoramic introduction, beginning with "Throughout the ages . . . ," for example, or "In today's society . . . ," teachers may fault the student for overgeneralization or lack of support. But a famous historian can make sweeping claims about the course of history without a lot of specific detail and without always quoting the opinions of other historians. Ethos makes a difference.

There are some specific strategies that can increase a writer's credibility. Whether we want to or not, in every act of communication we give an impression of ourselves. The key in arguing is to be in control as much as possible of how we present ourselves. We manage credibility by presenting ourselves in the best possible way, establishing a relationship with our audience that is appropriate for the situation.

STRATEGIES FOR ESTABLISHING ETHOS

SHARING PERSONAL INFORMATION

Trust can come from what we know about a speaker or writer: his or her position or role in the community, prior behavior, and knowledge or expertise. When analyzing ethos in a written argument, the first step is to consider a writer's background. If you don't know much about the writer, then consider the background information he or she reveals. Look for stories the writer tells or examples the writer gives from his or her own life. Look for information about the author provided by an editor. You might even do some research to find out even more about the author. Then consider the following questions:

What is the writer's standing in the community?

What position does he or she hold?

What kind of authority and influence come with this position?

What is the writer's reputation?

What is the writer's education, experience, or expertise?

What about the writer's life is particularly appropriate for the issue under discussion?

As you construct your own arguments, ask these questions about yourself and consider what information about your own life might be appropriate to share with your readers.

ADOPTING AN AUTHORITATIVE VOICE

Writers can also establish credibility through the way they present themselves. For instance, it is important for a job applicant to make a good impression through a resume and in an interview. Even if an applicant has experience, education, and expertise, if these qualities do not come through on the resume or during the interview, then the candidate won't be hired. In other words, it isn't enough to actually *know* what you're talking about; you also have to *sound* like you know.

Writers can sound credible by adopting an authoritative voice. This includes properly using the language of authority for whatever issue we are discussing. We trust doctors, educators, and other experts in part because they sound like experts. They speak the language of science and education, languages that our society recognizes as authoritative. If you want to sound knowledgeable about science, you need to accurately use the language of science. Experts also know how to support their claims with well-documented, appropriate evidence. Studies, expert opinion, and statistics are not just an important part of a logical argument; citing them can also establish credibility.

Writers can also assume an authoritative voice through a technique called "voice merging" (Miller, 1992, p. 5). Voice merging occurs when a writer quotes, paraphrases, or alludes to an authoritative voice or to a voice that represents the values of the community. By merging his or her voice with this authoritative voice, the writer adds that credibility to his own. A political speaker, for example, might quote Thomas Jefferson, James Madison, George Washington, or some other political hero to lend authority to the argument. A religious leader might quote the Bible or some other sacred text. Some writers quote or allude to the works of literary figures considered great or important: William Shakespeare, Charles Dickens, Toni Morrison, or others. Citing such authorities is more than mere decoration; it also lends credibility to the writer.

IDENTIFYING WITH THE READER

When analyzing written arguments, consider how writers convey or create credibility by identifying with the values of the community. When politicians show themselves with their families, playing football with a group of marines, hiking the Grand Canyon, or visiting a school or homeless shelter, they are trying to show that they identify themselves with the values of the community. A writer does the same thing by using recognizable examples, sharing personal information, or appealing to reasons that support community values.

Choosing the right words is another way to identify with the reader. We trust those who "speak our language." One who speaks the language of the community seems to belong. For example, Martin Luther King, Jr., when addressing the African-American community, spoke the language of that community, drawing upon his experience and training as a folk preacher. But when he addressed liberal white audiences, a main source of support for his campaign for civil rights, he adapted his language, drawing upon his university training. In both instances, he strengthened his credibility by speaking the language of the people he was addressing (Miller, 1992, pp. 9–12).

SELECTING AN APPROPRIATE POINT OF VIEW

Point of view refers to the relationship the writer tries to establish with his or her readers. A first-person point of view (using "I" or "we") can create an intimate, personal, and friendly relationship between writer and readers, but "I" also draws attention to the writer as an individual. Doing so can be useful when a writer has particular expertise or relevant personal experience, or when he or she can speak as a representative member of a group. Using "I" may not be as effective, however, on formal occasions or when the personal experience of the writer may appear irrelevant, limited, or biased. Some teachers believe that the first-person point of view is never appropriate in academic writing, but in recent years, more and more academic authors are using "I" when sharing relevant personal information. Using "we" emphasizes what a writer shares with readers, but "we" can also alienate people who feel that they share very little with the writer. Readers might also reject a writer who seems to be overly intimate in order to draw them in, like avoiding a stranger who insists on giving them a hug.

A second-person point of view (using "you") immediately gains a reader's attention, as when someone calls your name out in a crowd or looks directly into your eyes. The second-person point of view is often used in giving instructions or warnings, and it lends itself very well to giving commands. Used too much, it can make a writer appear dictatorial, preachy, or condescending. Using "you" can also create a distance between the writer and reader or put readers on the defensive, particularly when they have some doubts about the writer's claims or motives.

A third-person point of view (using "he," "she," "it," "they," or "one") gives a sense of objectivity and formality. The third-person point of view creates a distance between the writer, the reader, and the issue, and it can give the impression that the writer is a detached and unbiased observer. For this reason, scientists and scholars often use the third-person point of view. However, the third-person point of view can make a writer appear apathetic and impassive. (Point of view and levels of formality are discussed further in Chapter 8.)

GIVING A BALANCED PRESENTATION

Through their research social psychologists have discovered that we tend to trust someone who is apparently arguing against his or her own self-interest. Suppose, for example, that a convicted criminal was arguing that the judicial system is much too strict. Would you find that person credible? But what if that same person was arguing that the criminal justice system is much too lenient? By arguing that we should get tough on crime, the convicted criminal is arguing against his own apparent self-interest and for that reason may be more believable (Aronson, 1999, pp. 78–79). We also tend to be suspicious of people who are obviously trying to persuade us. A stockbroker who offers us a tip on a stock may just be trying to sell his or her services. But if we *overhear* that same stockbroker giving a tip to someone, we are more likely to believe the tip because it's not presented as part of a sales pitch (Aronson, 1999, pp. 80–81). This research suggests that if we want to have greater credibility, we should not give the impression that we are selling something or arguing in our own self-interest. One way to do this is to make sure that we give a balanced presentation, that we make it clear to the reader that we have considered and fairly presented all positions on a topic.

FALLACIES OF ETHOS

A **fallacy** is an argument that seems reasonable but isn't, an argument that is deceptive or manipulative in some way. Fallacies of ethos work in two ways. In the first case, a person misuses ethos by misrepresenting his or her authority. In this case, an author might try to win the trust of an audience by presenting himself or herself as knowledgeable, trustworthy, or interested, when in reality he or she is just trying to take advantage of the audience's trust. In the second case, an author might attack an individual who really is credible in order to destroy that individual's authority.

AD HOMINEM

The Latin phrase *ad hominem* means "to the person." This term refers to a personal attack that has nothing to do with the argument. Of course, questioning a person's character or credibility is not necessarily fallacious. It becomes so when the attack on a person's character is used as a distraction from the real issue. For instance, it would not be fallacious to attack a scientist's experimental results if you had reason to believe that he or she had falsified data. An attack would be fallacious, however, if you based your criticism on the fact that the scientist had a string of outstanding parking tickets.

Some politicians use personal attacks as part of their campaign strategy. This is called "negative campaigning" or "mudslinging." A politician may rake up an opponent's past behavior, even things the opponent did when he or she was quite young, looking for anything that might damage the opponent's public image. Sometimes, politicians will even point to the irresponsible behavior of an opponent's relatives (siblings, children, in-laws, cousins) as a way of attacking the candidate's current credibility. But such attacks have little to do with the candidate's actual qualifications.

GUILT BY ASSOCIATION

Guilt by association is an attack on an individual's credibility based upon that individual's association with a particular group. This fallacy usually works in this way. You generalize from the behavior of some members of the group to the group as a whole, stereotyping all members of the group, and then you identify the individual you are attacking with that group. Racial stereotyping is one type of guilt by association. For instance, a neighbor said he didn't like the fact that an Asian family had moved into our neighborhood because he had worked with some Chinese people and found them untrustworthy. He assumed that because he didn't trust some Chinese people, he couldn't trust anyone Chinese. He also assumed that anyone with Asian features must be Chinese. (This particular family was Laotian.)

POISONING THE WELL

A writer who "poisons the well" presents an argument in such a biased or emotional way that it is difficult for an opponent to respond without looking dishonest or immoral. This strategy is also meant as a distraction from the real issue and may involve personal attacks. Here's an example: "Of course, this liar will tell you that he didn't steal my stuff. You can't believe a thief. Go ahead and ask him; he'll deny it." How is the accused supposed to respond? The very act of asserting innocence in this case can be construed as a sign of guilt. The emotional and manipulative nature of the language in this case is a distraction from the real issue: who is guilty of stealing?

FALSE AUTHORITY

The fallacy of false authority occurs when an author tries to establish credibility without any real authority or when an audience is willing to listen to a person who is popular rather than one who is knowledgeable. Con men use the fallacy of false authority to trick people out of their money. Advertisements may also use false authorities, often by using celebrities to endorse various products. A basketball player may be an expert on athletic shoes, but is an athlete any more qualified than any other sweaty person to endorse deodorant? Does playing a doctor on a daytime soap opera qualify someone to endorse a particular medical product or service? Just because someone is an expert in one area doesn't make that person an expert in another. Having a Ph.D. in chemistry doesn't necessarily make you an expert on educational issues.

PATHOS: APPEALS TO EMOTION

In addition to gaining someone's trust, influencing your readers' emotions is also a powerful means of persuasion. Aristotle uses the Greek word *pathos*, which means "emotion," to describe a strategy of persuasion that appeals to the emotions. Overwhelming evidence from research shows that people are more likely to be persuaded if they are moved by a strong emotion, such as fear (Aronson, 1999, p. 85). In fact, although it isn't conclusive, there is some research that suggests that a message that is *primarily* emotional is more persuasive than a message that is *primarily* logical (Aronson, 1999, p. 84). This research suggests that even arguments that focus on logic will be more persuasive if they contain an emotional dimension. A logical argument may be convincing, but it won't usually be compelling. People may change their minds because of a logical argument, but pathos is more likely to cause them to change their behavior.

Although the Greek word *pathos* is the root for the English words *pathetic, empathy,* and *sympathy,* pathos concerns a much wider range of emotions than pity. In his *Art of Rhetoric,* Aristotle (1991) discusses anger and mildness; friendship and enmity; fear and boldness; shame and shamelessness; gratitude; pity and indignation; envy and emulation (pp. 122–162). A skillful writer can use fear, anger, humor, or compassion to put audience members in a particular emotional state such that they would receive a message that they might otherwise reject. Emotions literally put you in another state of mind. When people are afraid or in love, they may act in a way that to others might seem irrational. Because emotional arguments carry such power, you need to be careful how you use them and wary of how others may use them on you. As you analyze an author's appeal to emotions or when you find yourself responding emotionally to an argument, consider whether the emotions you are feeling are consistent with the issue and appropriate for the magnitude of the problem. As you compose your own arguments, you need to be responsible in how you appeal to others' emotions.

Emotional arguments can be found throughout an argument, but the direct emotional appeal is often stated near the beginning or the end. Placed at the beginning of an essay, an emotional argument can catch readers' interest and predispose them to read the argument with a favorable attitude. Placed at the end, an emotional appeal may move readers to action. Research suggests that strong emotion can be debilitating unless people are given some specific things they can do (Aronson, 1999, p. 87), so it would be appropriate at the end of an emotional argument to give readers something specific they can do to act on the emotion, such as a phone number they can call or website they can visit to register their opinion.

In most academic writing, the appeal to emotions is considered less convincing than ethos or logos, particularly when the appeal is exaggerated or manipulative. The academic community usually expects that any appeal to emotions will be used to reinforce a logical argument.

STRATEGIES FOR CREATING EMOTIONAL APPEAL

USING CONCRETE EXAMPLES

Concrete examples give an argument presence; they make an argument real and immediate for readers. Journalists recognize that running a photograph along with a news story makes the story more immediate. Showing a picture of a young child who has been kidnapped will create a much greater emotional response than merely reporting the child's kidnapping. Providing personal information about the child, showing her toys and family, or interviewing her classmates heightens the emotional response. A news story may contain statistics on how many families lack adequate food, shelter, or clothing, but few may respond. But if a reporter describes the plight of one particular family, then readers are more likely to help.

The emotional response created by a concrete example may make the difference between action and inaction. For example, on September 11, 2001, the nation watched in horror as a terrorist attack destroyed the twin towers of the World Trade Center in New York City, killing almost 3,000 people, including over 300 firefighters. The horror and emotion of the event were captured in Charles Porter's photo of firefighters carrying the limp body of Father Mychal Judge, chaplain of the New York City Fire Department, from the scene of devastation. This picture, and others like it, touched an emotional chord in the

American people because it put a human face on the tragedy, causing an outpouring of grief and sympathy.

Research by social psychologists shows that one powerful example can be much more persuasive than statistics. Even though studies and statistics may show that the Volvo is one of the safest and most reliable cars on the road, if your friend's cousin had a bad experience with a Volvo, you probably won't buy one. Even if a thousand people reported that they were satisfied with the Volvo, this one counterexample will carry more weight (Aronson, 1999, p. 90).

And the more vivid the example, the more persuasive it will be. Eliot Aronson (1999) conducted an experiment in which he worked with home auditors from utility companies to persuade consumers to add weather stripping to their homes to make their homes more energy efficient. One group offered statistics on the benefits of these improvements and met with little success. Only about 15 percent of homeowners agreed to make the improvements. A second group used a vivid example, explaining to homeowners that if they added up all of the cracks around all the doors and windows in their home, it would be the same as a hole in their exterior wall the size of a basketball. By using this example, auditors were able to convince 61 percent of homeowners to install weather stripping. This one vivid example made the difference (pp. 90–91).

Vivid examples come from vivid language. Instead of just telling readers how they should feel, writers try to re-create an emotional experience in such a way that readers actually do feel the associated emotion.

Word Choice

Word choice is also important in creating an emotional response. Some words carry more emotional weight than others. Writers need to pay particular attention to the connotations of words, their suggested or implied meanings, in addition to the denotative or dictionary meanings (see Chapter 5). For instance, the words *cheap* and *inexpensive* both have similar denotative meanings. They both refer to something that can be bought at a lower price than expected. However, *cheap* can carry a negative connotation of "lower quality" as well as "lower price." To say that a person is "cheap" means that he or she is careful with money but with the negative connotation of "miserly" or "stingy." More positive words with roughly the same denotation are "frugal" or "thrifty."

Some words carry such powerful emotional overtones that they color other terms that are associated with them. Richard Weaver (1985), a political philosopher, literary critic, and rhetorical theorist, calls such terms "ultimate terms" (pp. 211–212). These are highly emotional terms around which other terms cluster. Ultimate terms with a positive connotation Weaver calls "god terms" (1985, p. 212). Those with a negative connotation are called "devil terms" (1985, p. 222). For instance, in the 1950s and 1960s, *communism* was a devil term for many Americans. Anything or anyone associated with communism— even obliquely—was painted by anti-communists with the same broad brush. In the 1950s, at the height of the anti-communist crusade by Republican Senator Joseph McCarthy of Wisconsin, even the slightest association of a person with communism or left-wing politics could ruin that person's life. For more obvious reasons, the word *Nazi* is another example of a devil term. In our own time, *terrorism* has become a devil term. The following words would be god terms for many Americans: *democracy, liberty, family, prosperity*. When you analyze emotional language in an argument, check to see if these emotional words form a pattern or cluster of related terms that may be connected to an ultimate term, either a god term or a devil term.

Writers should also pay close attention to figurative language, such as metaphor, simile, analogy, allusion, imagery, hyperbole, understatement, personification, rhetorical questions, and irony, all of which are discussed in detail in Chapter 5. Figures of speech draw attention to themselves because they deviate from the expected. For instance, an environmental activist might refer to the clear-cutting of timber as the "rape of the earth." *Rape* is a highly emotional term with seriously negative connotations. It suggests violence and domination. Readers would have difficulty responding positively to a word such as *rape*. At the same time, the word *rape* is used metaphorically, and the comparison of clear-cutting with the act of rape is obviously meant to shock. The comparison is likewise an example of personification because rape is an attack by one person on another. Presenting the earth as a woman in this way may gain the unconscious sympathy of readers who feel for the victims of sexual violence. On the other side, supporters of clear-cutting might refer to this act as "harvesting," using a word that carries much more benign connotations. *Harvesting* suggests farming and gaining the benefits of one's own labors. It may also evoke the nostalgia and respect that many Americans have for the traditional farmer.

FALLACIES OF PATHOS

Emotions play an important role in persuasion, particularly in moving people to act on their convictions. But emotions can be easily manipulated as well. **Fallacies of pathos** occur when an author uses emotions to obscure an issue, divert attention away from the real issue, lead others into errors in reasoning, or exaggerate the significance of an issue. Teachers, for example, occasionally hear fallacious appeals to emotion from their students. I once had a student who missed a lot of class and skipped some major assignments. He turned in a final essay, but it showed signs of being thrown together at the last minute. When I told him he wouldn't be passing the class, he complained about how angry his parents would be if he lost his scholarship. His implied argument was this: "You should give me a passing grade because my parents will be angry with me if you don't." The assumption here is that performance in college courses should be measured by how parents will react to the final grades. This assumption was unacceptable to me, but the student was hoping that the vividness of his emotional appeal would distract me from the flimsiness of the argument.

Ad Populum

The Latin phrase "ad populum" means "to the people." The term refers to a fallacious argument that appeals to popular prejudices. One of these is the *bandwagon appeal*, an appeal to popularity—if everyone else is doing it, it must be right. Here are a couple of examples: "It is all right for me to cheat on my taxes because everyone else does it"; "It's all right for me to break the speed limit because I'm just keeping up with the flow of traffic. Besides, other people go faster than I do." The assumption in these arguments is that "just because something is popular or common practice, it must be right." Another ad populum fallacy is the *appeal to traditional wisdom.* This fallacy is an appeal to what has been done in the past: "That's just the way we've always done it." A related fallacy is the *appeal to provincialism,* the belief that the familiar is automatically superior to the unfamiliar: "That's just how it's done around here."

THREATS/REWARDS

The appeal to force is another name for a threat. A threat diverts attention from the real issue to the negative consequences of not accepting the argument. Extortion, blackmail, intimidation, hate speech, racial slurs, and sexual harassment are all examples of threats. The appeal to reward is just the opposite of a threat, diverting attention from the issue to what will be gained by accepting the point of view. Buying votes, trading favors, and bribery are all examples of the appeal to reward.

RED HERRING

The "red herring" fallacy probably takes its name from a trick once used by escaping prisoners: dragging a fish across their path of escape to throw dogs off the scent. A red herring is any attempt to draw attention away from the issue by raising irrelevant issues. This diversion often involves obscuring the issue with more emotional issues. Here is an example: "I don't think the president's economic plan is a good idea. I mean, what is he going to do about the violence in our inner cities?"

LOGOS: BUILDING LOGICAL ARGUMENTS

The Greek word *logos* has several different meanings. It can mean "word, thought, reason, or order." Our English word *logic* derives from *logos,* but logos has a broader meaning than logic. Logos refers to arguing through reasoning—the presentation of rational thought through language. Logos appeals to our ability to think; ethos and pathos typically work on our non-rational faculties, our abilities to trust and feel. Although ethos and pathos can be more compelling, logos provides the backbone of arguing, particularly for academic writing. Logos provides an overall framework of which ethos and pathos are a part. Arguments from ethos and pathos can be rationalized. In other words, they can be explained in terms of claims and reasons, but arguments from logos require claims and reasons as their basic structure. And although ethos and pathos are important to move people to action, it is logos that leads to conviction, to belief that lasts after the emotion passes. Logos protects us against illegitimate or manipulative uses of language and allows us to reflect on what we feel and what we believe. Although logos may not inspire people as much as ethos and pathos, logos will often prevent people from acting foolishly or rashly.

The power of reflection and contemplation associated with logos is what makes this appeal so important for academic writing. Academic authors typically value certainty, and they will usually approach conclusions tentatively until a preponderance of evidence convinces them that the conclusion is true or useful. This is why academic writers want to test one another's arguments and have their arguments tested by others. This is why scientists usually try to replicate the experiments of other scientists, why social scientists compare their data with the data of other social scientists, or why art critics will check an author's interpretation or evaluation of a work against their own. At its worst, academic argument can become as contentious and rancorous as any other argument. But at its best, academic argument leads to **critical thinking**, the ability to judge for ourselves the rightness of a claim based on the available evidence. Logos provides the key to this critical judgment.

When we supply reasons to support our opinions, we discover—perhaps for the first time—why we hold the opinions we do. We may also discover that some cherished opinions have no rational basis. In this way, logical argument and critical thinking not only create new knowledge, but they also can lead to self-knowledge, to a better understanding of who we are and what we believe. Critical thinking is part of the process of gaining an education. Through informed and responsible arguing, we recognize truths that would otherwise go unnoticed.

The process of testing ideas through logical argument is a particularly important part of a college education. According to the philosopher Richard Rorty (1999), a college serves two functions: providing students with "cultural literacy" and with "critical literacy" (pp. 114–126). **Cultural literacy** is an awareness of the common knowledge of the community of educated people. A degree in law or medicine, for example, certifies that the student who receives the degree has adequately learned the body of knowledge that scholars in the legal or medical communities value. But a university serves the additional function of teaching critical literacy. **Critical literacy** is the ability to question or explore what is believed to be true, to challenge or dispute the claims and opinions of others in an attempt to clarify and understand. Ideally, a college is a place where people can come together to ask questions, debate, and discuss ideas in a responsible fashion. This process of questioning and responding is critical thinking. It takes place primarily through language, through reading, writing, and speaking. Critical thinking can create tension, but it also represents the ideal for education.

STRATEGIES FOR CREATING LOGICAL APPEAL

So what makes a logical argument a good argument? Philosopher T. Edward Damer (2001) provides four criteria to use to evaluate arguments: **relevance**, **acceptability**, **sufficiency**, and **accountability** (pp. 23–31). These criteria are useful in analyzing arguments or in building your own.

RELEVANCE

First of all, an argument needs to be relevant. In other words, the reasons and assumptions offered need to relate to the issue being discussed. You can test the relevance of reasons and assumptions by asking yourself, "If these reasons and assumptions are true, would I be more or less likely to believe the truthfulness of the claims?" If you would be less likely to be convinced, then there is a good chance that the reasons are irrelevant. Testing the relevance of an argument is also a good way to check for manipulative uses of ethos and pathos (Damer, 2001, p. 24). If authority and emotion aren't really relevant to the argument, then you can set these aside and focus on the heart of the argument.

ACCEPTABILITY

In the process of analyzing arguments, you may begin to think that any claim can be called into question. In addition, reasons and assumptions can themselves become claims in need of additional support, leading to a chain of reasoning with no apparent solid intellectual ground upon which you can build with any certainty. Where does the justifying of claims, reasons, and assumptions come to an end? Couldn't a stubborn person keep asking for more and more support, disputing every statement in an argument, continually asking—as a young child does—"Why? Why? Why?" If one wants to be stubborn, yes; but such orneriness becomes ridiculous after a while. When arguments have a context, when they are a meaningful part of the life of a community, then at some point they can be grounded in what the community accepts as credible, authoritative, or true—the common sense or common knowledge of the community. This stock of knowledge differs from one community to another, and not all members of any group completely agree on what constitutes "common knowledge." This is why disagreements arise in the first place. But still there are statements and beliefs that most members of a community accept as true, and an argument will be persuasive only when the reasons and assumptions that justify the claim are grounded in the common beliefs of the community. Reasons that are grounded in the common beliefs of the community are called "community-based reasons."

One danger in relying on community-based reasons and adapting your argument to the needs of your audience is that you may compromise the integrity of your own views. In other words, you may end up just telling people what they want to hear. But it doesn't have to be this way. The reasons you choose to justify your argument may not be the most compelling reasons for you, but they may be the most convincing for those you are addressing. And if you can still accept these reasons, you preserve your integrity.

I once had a student writing an essay about a controversy in the small town she came from. A town ordinance forbade the consumption and sale of alcohol in city parks. Some citizens wanted to change the ordinance to make the sale and consumption of alcohol legal by special permit. The intent of this proposed change was to make it possible for the town to attract concerts to the city parks, which many believed would help the town's economy. At the same time, influential religious groups in the town opposed the change because public drinking violated their religious beliefs or because they believed that such easy access to alcohol would destroy the moral fiber of the town, making it an unhealthy place to raise a family. These groups argued that giving in on this drinking law would open the door to all kinds of compromises in the name of economic development.

The issue had polarized the town. Supporters of the change saw members of the religious groups as being self-righteous and judgmental or as trying to protect their own interests. When my student wrote her discovery draft (her argument for herself), she sided with those who objected to the proposed change on religious and moral grounds. But she realized that because the town was so polarized, these reasons might not be convincing to the community as a whole or to the town council.

Being an emergency room nurse at the local hospital, which was in a neighboring city that did allow the sale of alcohol for park concerts, she knew that on concert nights the emergency room was overloaded with concert-goers who had had too much to drink or had run into trouble with those who had. Her own son even had to wait for emergency medical care on a concert night. So in her next draft, she argued that allowing alcohol at concerts in her town—in addition to the neighboring town—would overload the local medical system and ultimately cost much more in human and monetary terms than it would gain.

Even though this was not the most compelling reason for my student, it was a reason that she nonetheless believed in strongly and one that added a new dimension to the debate, an argument centered in the common values of the community. After all, who would deny the value of reliable medical care?

So how can you increase the probability that the reasons you offer will be acceptable to your audience? Damer (2001) suggests several ways:

- Build your argument on accepted common knowledge or shared beliefs and values.

- Draw upon your own experience and observation.

- Develop a chain of reasoning by building on the conclusions of other good arguments.

- Draw upon undisputed eyewitness testimony or expert opinion. (p. 26)

SUFFICIENCY

According to Damer (2001), there aren't clear-cut guidelines for determining sufficiency. You just need to ensure that your argument has enough reasons and assumptions with enough weight to be convincing to your argument. As a general rule, anecdotal evidence is not enough. And a single example, although it may be vivid, usually isn't adequate to support a point. Because they can be tested by rigorous statistical methods, studies of various kinds usually provide strong support for an argument (p. 28). One way to ensure that you have sufficient evidence is to engage in a dialogue with others. Ask, "What kind of evidence or what amount of evidence would you require to accept this claim?" Determining sufficiency comes with experience and where there aren't established guidelines, it usually needs to be negotiated.

ACCOUNTABILITY

I have used the term *accountability* to describe what Damer (2001) calls "the rebuttal principle." According to this principle, an argument should be able to offer an effective response to any other possible arguments (p. 29). In other words, an argument needs to be accountable to other perspectives, to counterarguments, and counterexamples. Some writers may think that by revealing to their readers other perspectives on an issue they may weaken their argument, but the opposite is true—if they can give a reasonable response to these other arguments. If you really can't answer other arguments, then perhaps it's time to reconsider your position.

FALLACIES OF LOGOS

Logical fallacies are arguments that look rational, fair, and valid, but aren't. If you take a logic class, you will learn a lot about formal fallacies—arguments that don't follow the proper form of a logical syllogism (see Chapter 2). The following are common informal fallacies: errors in reasoning related to claims, reasons, and assumptions.

BEGGING THE QUESTION

You "beg the question" when you offer a reason that is really just a restatement of the conclusion. For example, "You should exercise because it's good for you" is just another way of saying "You should exercise because you should exercise." That is, it begs readers to ask, "How is exercise good for me?" A writer also begs the question when he or she offers a conclusion without adequate support or uses reasons or assumptions that are just as controversial as the conclusion. Consider the following familiar argument: "Abortion is wrong because it is murder." This argument doesn't really advance the conversation about abortion because it offers as a reason one of the primary points of contention in the abortion issue: is a fetus really an individual human life that can be "murdered"?

COMPLEX QUESTION

A complex or "loaded" question is really two questions phrased as one. A famous example is "Have you stopped beating your wife?" The two questions phrased here as one are "Have you ever beaten your wife?" and "If so, have you stopped?" As the question is phrased, answering either "yes" or "no" will get a husband in trouble: "Yes (I used to beat her, but I stopped)"; "No (I still beat her)." Another famous example is this: "Are you aware that your tie clashes with your suit?" The introductory phrases "Are you aware . . ." or "Did you know . . ." usually signal a complex question.

EQUIVOCATION

Equivocation is using one term for two different definitions. When using this fallacy, an author will often have one definition in mind while allowing the audience to think that he or she means something else. When President Clinton was asked about his relationship with Monica Lewinsky, he insisted that he did not have "sexual relations" with "that woman." Many Americans accused him of equivocating in this case with the commonplace definition of "sexual relations" or the identity of "that woman."

HASTY GENERALIZATION/SWEEPING GENERALIZATION

A hasty generalization is another name for "jumping to conclusions." It is a conclusion formed on scant evidence. Here is an example: "They laid off five people at work today. That probably means the country is going into recession." The assumption in this argument is that a few people being laid off at one office is a sure sign of a coming recession. But the economy is so large and complex that five people being laid off at one office would have no effect. This conclusion requires more evidence.

A sweeping generalization is similar to a hasty generalization. It involves applying a statement that is true for one particular situation to another situation without considering how the two situations may differ. Here is an example: "My accounting degree really prepared me well for law school. Everyone who wants to go to law school should major in accounting." The assumption in this argument is that what is true for the writer is true for everyone. The argument ignores important differences among students. Some people feel well prepared for law school after studying English, political science, or philosophy.

FALSE ANALOGY

An analogy is a powerful persuasive tool because it presents an argument in interesting and memorable terms. Analogies provide the assumptions that ground many arguments. An analogy becomes fallacious, however, when the differences between the things compared are greater than the similarities. When the United States became involved in wars against communists in Korea and Vietnam, government leaders justified their actions by referring to the "domino theory." According to this theory, if communists were allowed to take over one country, neighboring countries would also fall to communism like a line of dominoes, risking world domination by communist nations. This analogy is a powerful and memorable image, but it ignores the fact that international politics is much more complex than stacking dominoes. The domino theory was also based on the assumption that Asian nations were like European nations in their politics and that one Asian nation (Korea) was pretty much like another (Vietnam). These assumptions proved to be false as well.

Post Hoc

The full Latin name for this fallacy is *post hoc, ergo propter hoc,* a phrase that means "after this, therefore because of this." This fallacy refers to an error in reasoning based on the assumption that just because one event follows another, the first caused the second. A lot of superstitions originate in this fallacy. A person walks under a ladder and a bucket of paint falls on his head, so he tells people that walking under a ladder brings bad luck. The problem is that walking under the ladder didn't cause the bucket to fall (unless he bumped the ladder); further, to jump to the conclusion that there is a connection between ladders and bad luck is a hasty generalization. Buckets don't fall every time someone walks under a ladder. We just remember the times they do.

Slippery Slope

The slippery slope is another fallacy of causality. It occurs when you argue that one event will inevitably lead through a series of related events resulting in disaster. It's found in the familiar warning given to kids: "If you steal a candy bar, then you will steal toys, then bikes, then cars, and then you'll find yourself on death row." It is true that most criminals started with petty crimes, but it isn't true that every kid who steals a candy bar will turn into a murderer. This argument is just designed to scare kids; logically, it doesn't work. The slippery slope fallacy is a favorite of political extremists who argue that voting for one candidate (or the other) will drive the country to ruin. It is true that voting has consequences, but a lot of other decisions would have to be made before an individual could ruin the government. You'll hear extremists argue that one particular bill, this one Supreme Court nominee, or just a slight increase in taxes will all bring the country to unavoidable disaster. Of course, fatal decisions can be made, but as with any causal argument, the writer should be prepared to explain exactly how the causal chain works.

OVERSIMPLIFICATION

Oversimplification occurs when a writer makes an argument that reduces complex issues to a simple argument. An oversimplification may have some truth, but because it leaves out important information, it is misleading. Here is an example: "Jogging is good for you. Everybody ought to jog every day." It may be true—*all other things being equal*—that jogging is good for you, but some people may have conditions that make jogging harmful or inappropriate. One kind of oversimplification is *oversimplified cause*. This fallacy occurs when a writer tries to reduce a complex event or phenomenon to one simple cause, such as arguing that school violence is caused by video games. These may contribute to violence among *some* students, but a complex issue such as school violence can't be reduced to such a simple cause. Because causality typically involves complex relationships, the oversimplified cause is quite common.

STACKING THE DECK

Gamblers "stack the deck" in their favor by arranging the cards so that they will win. Writers "stack the deck" by ignoring any evidence or arguments that don't support their position. For example, a drug company might stack the deck by releasing only the positive results of experiments on a new drug, suppressing any negative results. I once experienced "stacking the deck" when buying a used car. The person trying to sell me the car talked about how wonderful the car was. After I bought the car, the person trying to sell me an extended warranty pointed out all the things that could go wrong with the car. In both cases, these sales representatives were stacking the deck by ignoring either the good or bad qualities of the car. Whenever you're hearing only one side of a story, you should wonder what's being left out.

APPEAL TO IGNORANCE

The burden of supporting an argument falls on the person making it. A writer who makes an appeal to ignorance refuses to accept this burden of proof and tries to use the lack of evidence *as* evidence to support a claim. Here is an example: "Bigfoot, the Loch Ness monster, and extraterrestrials must really exist because no one has ever proved they don't." In fact, those who make the claim "Bigfoot exists" are the ones who need to support the claim. It would be a mistake, however, to assume that "Bigfoot doesn't exist" just because you don't have evidence that he does. "Bigfoot doesn't exist" is also a claim that requires support.

NON SEQUITUR

The Latin phrase *non sequitur* means "it does not follow." This refers to a conclusion that has no apparent connection to the reasons. Non sequiturs are often used in advertising. For example, a car may be pictured with a beautiful woman draped across the hood, the implied argument being "Look at this beautiful woman. You should buy this car." But there is no clear connection between the conclusion and the reason. The woman is just there to get your attention. It is not possible to identify a set of assumptions or reasons that would link the reason and conclusion in a sensible way.

FALSE DILEMMA

The false dilemma, or "either/or" fallacy, involves trying to force readers to accept a conclusion by presenting only two options, one of which is clearly more desirable than the other. Rarely are there only two positions on any issue. I have to admit, however, that my wife and I have used this strategy on our kids: "Do you want to get started on your homework or piano lessons first?" "Hard-sell" salespersons and negotiators often use the false dilemma to close a deal, to get people to say "yes": "Do you want to pay cash or credit for that?" (eliminating the option that you might not want to buy it at all); "If you don't act now, you'll never get another chance"; "Would you rather buy whole-life insurance or risk leaving your family without an income?"

STRAWPERSON

Imagine how much easier it would be to knock over a scarecrow than a real person. The strawperson is an oversimplified and distorted version of another's viewpoint that is easy to refute. A writer usually resorts to setting up a strawperson when his or her own arguments are not particularly convincing. In such a case, the writer has to weaken the other point of view to the point that it can be easily challenged. The strawperson works best when the other person is unable to respond or give a proper account of his or her own viewpoint.

CONCLUSION

As Aristotle makes clear in his definition of rhetoric, there is a power that comes from knowing how to identify and use means of persuasion. Once you learn what they are, you will see them in use all around you. Although there are many specific techniques for how to build credibility, create emotion, or build logical arguments, focusing on these broad strategies can make you a more effective communicator and help you to develop your own beliefs and values.

REFERENCES

Aristotle. (1991). *On rhetoric: A theory of civic discourse.* G.A. Kennedy (Ed. & Trans.), New York: Oxford University Press.

Aronson, E. (1999). *The social animal.* New York: Worth Publishers.

Damer, T. E. (2001). *Attacking faulty reasoning.* Belmont, CA: Wadsworth.

Miller, K. (1992). *Voice of deliverance: The language of Martin Luther King, Jr. and its sources.* New York: The Free Press.

Reiner, R. (Director). (1995). *The American president.* [Film]. United States: Castle Rock.

Rorty, R. (1999). *Philosophy and social hope.* London: Penguin.

Weaver, R. (1985). *The ethics of rhetoric.* Davis, CA: Hermagoras Press.

NOTES

NOTES

NOTES

Chapter 5

THE POWER OF
THE WORD

Brett C. McInelly

INTRODUCTION

A few years ago while reading a student paper on the role sex education should play in public schools, I encountered a revealing statement. In documenting statistics regarding the percentage of young adults who have their first sexual experience during their high-school years, the student author writes, "By the time they reach high-school age, an average of 90% of the teenage boys have had sex, while 70% of the girls have lost their virginity" (Batchelor, 1994, p. 32). Although the percentages may be startling to some readers, I found the language the writer uses to be far more striking: boys "have" sex; girls "lose" their virginity! I suspect the student didn't think much about the distinction she was making in choosing to characterize in different terms the same event—the "first sexual encounter" for boys and girls. In fact, I wonder if the words weren't used unconsciously on the student's part. What the words reveal, however, are two very different attitudes regarding gender and sex. The first phrase is relatively positive—to "have" something is generally good—and indicates that boys are active; to "have" something suggests that one has taken possession of it. Girls, on the other hand, are portrayed as passive, since something (their virginity) is taken from them. The second phrase likewise portrays the first sexual experience as negative, since losing something is generally bad. While the student author probably didn't intentionally mean what the words imply, her language projects the idea that boys having sex is more acceptable than girls losing their virginity.

The student's word choice indicates something of the power of language: words reveal our attitudes, values, and perceptions of the world. While societal attitudes and values certainly change over time, it is fair to say that, historically, our society has had (and perhaps still does) a double standard regarding sex. Our culture has been much more accepting of sexually-active men than sexually-active women. In high school a sexually-active young man is often admired by his peers, whereas a sexually-active young woman is branded as "easy," perhaps even called a "slut." I wonder if this attitude doesn't carry into adulthood as well. What seems clear to me is the language the student author uses—to "have" and to "lose"—indicates this double standard, even if the student didn't consciously mean to suggest it. Her words reveal something of her and her culture's attitudes and values.

But language just doesn't provide a looking glass into our attitudes and values; it shapes those things as well. I would argue, in fact, that language even shapes our sense of reality. After all, the student author didn't coin the two phrases she uses to describe the first sexual experience for boys and girls. The words are ones she likely picked up in conversation, through the media, and in reading, and they've influenced the way she (and all of us) think and talk about sex. Consider, for example, what or whom you think of when you hear the word "virgin." I suspect that most of us immediately think of a female, perhaps one we imagine as pure and innocent; we generally don't think of an innocent young man. The word "virgin," then, influences the way we think about and the values we assign to women and sexual activity.

The point is that words both reveal and shape the way we look at the world, and this is important to understand when crafting an argument and deciding on what words will help us achieve a desired effect with our audience. If our goal is to influence, language is the principal means by which we will influence our audience. And since others are daily trying to influence us, we should be sensitive to the ways language works when analyzing arguments.

THE SOPHISTS

Early rhetoricians understood the power of words, and they spent a lot of time thinking about the nature of language and its effect on our perceptions of reality. In fifth-century Athens, a group of rhetoricians, known as sophists, focused much of their attention on the power of language and developed some of the earliest theories regarding the nature of language. One of their main motivations for studying the way language influences an audience resides in the fact that these men made their living by teaching rhetoric; sophists were teachers of argument. And they were in high demand, since being an active and influential citizen in Athenian society required a mastery of the rhetorical arts. In civic and legal life, individual citizens generally represented their own interests. There were no lawyers, so if someone brought a legal suit against you, you prepared and made your own defense. If you wanted to influence public policy, you made your case in the public square. To refine your rhetorical skills, you would likely solicit the services of a sophist to train you in how to make an effective argument.

While the sophists provided a needed service, they were not universally liked nor were their services always appreciated. Philosophers like Plato distrusted them, in part, because they believed the sophists taught their pupils to use rhetoric to manipulate audiences and distort the truth. From Plato's point of view, the sophists were less interested in the truth or facts of a case than they were in teaching people to win an argument at any cost. In short, Plato took a more idealistic view of things, whereas the sophists were a bit more pragmatic: for Plato absolute truth was the bottom line; for the sophists truth was relative or whatever you could convince your audience to believe. But both Plato and the sophists recognized that language has a powerful effect on audiences. As one fifth-century sophist explains, "Just as different drugs draw forth different humors from the body—some putting a stop to disease, others to life—so too with words: some cause pain, others joy, some strike fear, some stir the audience to boldness, some benumb and bewitch the soul with evil persuasion" (Gorgias, 2001, p. 32). Plato distrusted rhetoric because language could have this kind of effect; the sophists accepted the fact and sought out effective ways of influencing audiences.

Plato's trouble with the sophists partly explains why, historically, sophists have been given a bad rap. Curiously, the word "sophist" derives from the same root as the Greek words *sophos* and s*ophia*, which mean "wise" and "wisdom" respectively (Kerferd, 1981, p. 24). Hence, a sophist was originally one possessing wisdom. However, today the phrase "sophistry"—as in the statement, "That's just sophistry"—is used to describe confusing and illogical arguments, or linguistic trickery. And Plato was right to some extent: language can distort the truth and manipulate an audience. If people are using words in ways that seem dishonest or unethically calculating, we might (and probably should) call them on it. We also should avoid using language in such ways when making our own arguments. At the same time, we should be conscious of the lessons about language the sophists taught, recognizing that the words we use impact our attempts to influence an audience. We, of course, want to be responsible, but we should also be strategic in the words we choose to make a point. In most cases, the right word or words make or break an argument.

In short, whether as rhetors or auditors (i.e., one who reads/hears an argument), we need to be aware of the nuances of language and understand that language both reveals and shapes perceptions of the world and of the issues we debate in public and private life. Developing this awareness involves understanding diction (or word choice), figurative language, and tone.

DICTION

When looking at diction, we need to recognize that words aren't neutral; that is, words aren't merely tools we use to communicate what we want to say. Although words certainly enable us to communicate with each other, we need to be attuned to the meaning that is implied in the words we choose to discuss particular matters or issues. We need to understand that a word can have a variety of meanings depending on the context in which it is used. For example, if my son, in referring to a passing automobile, exclaims to his best friend, "That's a killer car," his friend knows exactly what he means—that the car is especially stylish. If he were to make the same statement to his grandfather, his grandfather may not understand what he means by "killer." His grandfather might assume that the car is unsafe, either to the driver or to other drivers or pedestrians. This is because the word "killer" literally means someone or something that kills, but within the context of my son's statement, it means something else entirely.

This example illustrates what we mean by denotation and connotation. **Denotation** refers to the literal meaning of a word; **connotation** refers to all the other implications or associations we attach to a word. "Cool," for example, literally means moderately cold, but if my son had described the car by referring to it as "cool," he would have meant something similar to what he intended with the word "killer." Depending on how and in what situation a word is used, its meaning often varies.

Political pollsters, not unlike the ancient sophists, understand that the right word or words are essential to an effective argument, and they spend much of their time studying the ways voters respond to particular words and the meanings they affix to those words. They know that the words politicians use to frame their positions on particular issues are as important (if not more so) than the stance they take on those issues. One such pollster named Frank Luntz regularly conducts focus groups with voters to determine the associations people make with particular words in order to advise his clients—Republican politicians. In one such group, he asked a group of middle-class voters what they thought of when they heard the word "government." Their responses were revealing: "Controlling," "Bureaucracy," "Corruption," and "Liars." What Luntz discovered is that, in the minds of many voters, "government" has a negative connotation. Hence, he advises his clients to claim they are for "less government" and to accuse Democrats of wanting "more government" in American life (LeMann, 2000, pp. 104–105). Rather than refer to "global warming," he advises politicians to speak of "climate change." Why? Both phrases ostensibly describe the same phenomenon, but the second phrase is not nearly as threatening or ominous as the first; the first phrase has a much more negative connotation (LeMann, 2000, p. 100).

Part of Luntz's point is that words shape the way people think about and respond to particular issues. Luntz advises Republicans to talk about "tax relief" instead of "tax cuts" (LeMann, 2000, p. 100). In this case, "tax cuts" doesn't necessarily have a negative connotation; rather, "tax relief" frames the issue in such a way as to suggest that citizens are overburdened by taxes and in need of "relief." The phrase "tax relief" thus produces a stronger emotional response, since many Americans feel like they are overtaxed, and, from Luntz's point of view, the phrase is a more effective way of marshalling support for initiatives to reduce taxes. Luntz also found that many voters are more inclined to do away with a "death tax," whereas they were much more supportive of an "estate tax." Curiously, both phrases describe the same thing, so why is the former less appealing than the latter? The word "estate" is associated with wealth and prosperity; people tend to think that only the rich have "estates," and most middle-class voters aren't opposed to taxing the wealthy. "Death tax," on the other hand, sounds "unfair": "You work hard your whole life and the government takes it all away at the end" (LeMann, 2000, p. 105). What Luntz tries to get across to his clients is that the language they use to discuss issues shapes voters' perceptions and that getting elected or advancing public policy depends on a politician's rhetoric, not just his or her stance on the issues (LeMann, 2000, p. 109).

Luntz and others who provide this kind of advice have been criticized for what appears to some people as a manipulative way of using language to achieve political aims. Like the sophists, they're accused of disregarding the truth or facts of a situation, relying instead on linguistic tricks to represent an issue in the most politically advantageous way possible. These critics' accusations aren't entirely unfounded. Politicians certainly have been known to use language in deceptive ways. During his first presidential campaign in 1988, George Bush, Sr. made a statement that some analysts would later argue cost him the White House in 1992. In a speech at the Republican National

Convention, he said, "Read my lips: no new taxes." When taxes were raised during his presidency, Bush's critics charged him with lying to win the election. In his defense, Bush insisted that the government hadn't created "new" taxes but had merely raised existing ones. Democrats then accused Bush of equivocating—intentionally using one phrase with at least two different meanings—to win votes. When voters heard Bush claim there would be "no new taxes," they assumed taxes wouldn't be raised; when taxes were raised and Bush offered his defense, many citizens felt as if Bush had been intentionally deceptive.

Language thus can be used in questionable and potentially unethical ways, and we need to be aware of this when weighing the merits of an argument. When making arguments of our own, our aim hopefully isn't to mislead our audience or misrepresent the facts. At the same time, we need to recognize that an effective argument requires the right words as well as the right stuff or substance. The way our argument is perceived by an audience is strongly affected by our language and the associations readers make with the words we use. Consider, for example, the abortion debate. Those against abortion claim to be "pro-life"; those in favor of it claim to be "pro-choice." Both phrases ostensibly have a positive connotation. Who, after all, isn't an advocate for "life" or "choice?" Pro-life advocates certainly wouldn't say they are, at least in a general sense, opposed to the freedom to choose, and pro-choice advocates wouldn't say they're in favor of death or murder. Each group has chosen a phrase that frames their position in positive terms, and I don't think either phrase is intended to deliberately misrepresent the respective positions on the issue. Rather, they've chosen phrases that are rhetorically effective. This should be our goal when choosing the words to make our arguments.

FIGURATIVE LANGUAGE

Diction, then, is a powerful feature of an argument. So too is figurative language. Figurative language enables us to make our points in particularly memorable and meaningful ways. In a nutshell, **figurative language** involves using one thing or idea to represent another. Perhaps the most common example is the metaphor, which in the original Greek meant to "transfer."

Essentially, a **metaphor** is a comparison in which you "transfer" the meaning of one thing or object to another. For example, when Forrest Gump says, "Life is like a box of chocolates," he is using a **simile**, which is a type of metaphor using "like" or "as"; he is "transferring" the associations we make with eating a box of chocolates to life. By so doing, he is suggesting that life is unpredictable and full of surprises ("You never know what you're going to get").

So why not just say, "Life is full of surprises"? Why bother using a metaphor? In this particular case, I would argue that the metaphor is more memorable and makes the point more effectively because eating a box of chocolates is something most of us can relate to. Most of us have had the experience of choosing a chocolate. When surveying the box, all the chocolates look delicious, but we know from experience that not all the chocolates are equally satisfying to our own individual tastes. Sometimes we make a choice we are happy with; other times we are disappointed and wish we would have chosen a different one. Sometimes we don't get the one we had hoped for, but we are pleasantly surprised with the result. The point is we can never be sure of the outcome, but we have to make a choice nonetheless. According to Forrest, the experience of choosing a chocolate is a lot like the choices we make in life, and the metaphor is a particularly poignant way of making his point.

Let's consider a more elaborate metaphor. In the novel *A Farewell to Arms* by Ernest Hemingway, the main character finds himself sitting in a hospital waiting room at the end of the narrative. An ambulance driver in Italy during World War I, he has abandoned his post (hence, *A Farewell to Arms*) and run away to Switzerland with the woman he loves, a nurse. She has just delivered a stillborn baby and is about to die herself from complications associated with the delivery. As the main character recognizes that he has lost a child and will soon lose the woman he loves, he reflects on the nature of life and death. He has seen firsthand the brutality of war and human existence, and he eventually adopts a rather pessimistic worldview he describes in the following metaphor:

Once in camp I put a log on top of the fire and it was full of ants. As it commenced to burn, the ants swarmed out and went first toward the centre where the fire was; then turned back and ran toward the end. When there were enough on the end they fell off into the fire. Some got out, their bodies burnt and flattened, and went off not knowing where they were going. But most of them went toward the fire and then back toward the end and swarmed on the cool end and finally fell off into the fire. I remember thinking at the time that it was the end of the world and a splendid chance to be a messiah and lift the log off the fire and throw it out where the ants could get off onto the ground. But I did not do anything but throw a tin cup of water on the log, so that I would have the cup empty to put whiskey in before I added water to it. I think the cup of water on the burning log only steamed the ants. (pp. 327–328)

From the point of view of the main character, the experience of the ants parallels our own, in that we lead a harsh and seemingly senseless existence. If we survive, we do so only after experiencing great hardship and pain. This is certainly how the main character feels in the wake of losing his child and the woman he loves, to say nothing of the many friends he's seen die in battle. The experience of watching the ants on the log also reflects his thoughts regarding God. If a god does exist, the metaphor suggests that he looks on human suffering with little or no sympathy and does not intervene on our behalf. The metaphor of the ants on the log is thus an effective way for Hemingway to communicate to his readers a particular worldview and is certainly more effective than just saying that we live in a cruel and godless universe.

The metaphor is just one example of what is known as a figure of speech. In our language, there are literally hundreds of figures of speech, too many to be addressed comprehensively here. The important thing is to recognize when people are using language figuratively and to grasp the implications of a figure of speech. We also want to refine our ability to use figurative language in rhetorically effective ways. To assist you in recognizing and using figures of speech, here is a list of some of the more common figures, in addition to metaphor and simile, you will encounter in arguments.

Analogy: a kind of comparison in which something unfamiliar is explained by a comparison to something more familiar. In arguing that public-school curricula should include the study of religion, Warren A. Nord (2002) makes the following analogy: "For some time now, people have rightly argued that ignoring black history and women's literature (as texts and curricula have traditionally done) has been anything but neutral. Rather, it betrays a prejudice; it is discriminatory. And so it is with religion" (p. 174). Most people recognize that black history and the contributions of women to literature have not been given their due in public education, but most people do not recognize that, at least according to Nord, religion has been similarly marginalized.

Allusion: a reference to a historical event or person. Allusions are also made to events and persons from literature and other media (film, television, etc.). For example, Martin Luther King, Jr. begins his "I Have a Dream" speech with an allusion to Abraham Lincoln's "Gettysburg Address": "Five score years ago, a great American, in whose symbolic shadow we stand, signed the Emancipation Proclamation." In alluding to the opening of Lincoln's speech ("Four score and seven years ago . . .") King indirectly suggests that he is a modern-day Lincoln in his championing of civil rights while simultaneously paying homage to a revered American leader.

Imagery: particularly vivid language that evokes a mental image of what is being described. Imagery often encourages an emotional response. In decrying the practice of parents who withhold medical treatment from their children on religious grounds (Christian Science, for example, advocates faith healing in place of medical treatment), Rita Swan (2002) uses vivid imagery to portray the suffering of one child who died of bone cancer: "the tumor on her leg was more than forty inches in circumference and her genitalia were partially rotted away from lying in her own excrement" (p. 147).

Overstatement: also known as hyperbole, overstatement is the use of exaggeration to make a point. I have a friend who, upon entering a particularly chilly room, will exclaim, "You could store meat in here!" He is clearly exaggerating, but his statement effectively emphasizes how cold the room is.

Understatement: to state or represent something in terms that do not fully encapsulate its magnitude. If I accidentally touch a hot stove and my wife asks, "Was it hot?" I might respond by saying, "Just a bit," as I hurry to the freezer for an ice cube. By stating the opposite of what I mean, my wife understands exactly that the stove was, in fact, hot. As with overstatement, understatement can be an effective way to make a point.

Personification: giving human characteristics to animals, abstract ideas, and inanimate objects. As described in Chapter 4, referring to the clear-cutting of forests as a "rape of the earth" personifies the earth as a victim of violence.

Rhetorical Question: a stated question that does not necessitate a reply or answer. Such questions often have strong rhetorical effect. A politician mustering support for the War on Terror might string together a series of questions to rally support: "Don't all Americans want freedom? Don't we all want democracy? We can't have freedom or democracy until terrorism is a thing of the past."

Irony: saying one thing but meaning the opposite. In *A Modest Proposal*, the eighteenth-century author, Jonathan Swift, suggests that the Irish breed and then rear children, like cattle, for food for the English. Swift's intention isn't to encourage people to accept an outrageous proposal; rather, he hopes to draw attention through irony to English exploitation of the Irish. From his point of view, this exploitation is as bad or worse than his proposal.

DICTION AND FIGURATIVE LANGUAGE AT WORK IN AN ARGUMENT

To illustrate the ways figurative language, along with diction, work in an argument, let's look at a passage from an article drawing attention to the violent nature of the turtle-farming industry:

> Before being killed and canned, the turtles swim in dense kraals, bumping each other in the murky water, armor clashing, dully lurching against high pens. Later, trussed on a plank dock, they lie unblinking in the sun, their flippers pierced and tied. The tough leather of their skins does not disguise their present helplessness and pain. They wear thick, sun-hardened accumulations of blood at their wounds. Barbados turtles, as large as children, they belong to a species which has been eliminated locally by ardent harvesting off the waters near Key West, but the commercial tradition still brings them here to be slaughtered. Crucified like thieves, they breathe in little sighs, they gulp, they wait.
>
> At a further stage, in the room where the actual slaughtering occurs, the butchers stride through gore in heavy boots. The visitor must proceed on a catwalk; a misstep will plunge him into a slow river of entrails and blood. (Gold, 2002, p. 219)

You may have noticed the two similes—"as large as children" and "Crucified like thieves." The first is also an example of personification, humanizing the turtles and suggesting their helpless condition; the second emphasize their pain, since most people understand that the Roman practice of crucifixion was an extremely agonizing form of execution. The reference to crucifixion also makes an allusion to Jesus Christ, since most people are aware that Christ was crucified. The implication here is that the turtles, like Christ, are innocent victims of the brutality of others. The imagery ("murky water," "dully lurching," "sun-hardened accumulations of blood," "a slow river of entrails and blood," etc.) enables the reader to visualize the horrific nature of the scene. These elements combine to create a strong emotional appeal (pathos).

The diction is likewise effective in establishing the passage's persuasive appeal. Note that the turtles are "killed," not harvested. "Killed," of course, has a negative connotation, emphasizing the brutality of the practice and the innocence of the turtles. And the workers are not "farmers"; they are "butchers." Of course, one meaning of "butcher" is one who cuts or processes meat, so the term is accurate. But within the context of the passage, it is intended to portray these workers as the perpetrators of the turtles' misery. They are essentially portrayed as callous murderers.

TONE

The written word often projects the mood or attitude of the writer toward the subject or the audience. This is what we mean by **tone**. Tone is also a characteristic or attribute of voice (see Chapter 8). When speaking, we project our mood or attitude through body language, inflections in our voice, and so forth. When writing, tone is primarily created through our word choice, and as with speaking, our mood or attitude can be characterized in a number of ways: formal or casual, serious or playful, earnest or sarcastic, reasonable or angry, and on and on. In other words, we can project the full range of human emotions and attitudes in the language we use to discuss a topic. Consider the following examples, the first from an argument in support of prayer in school and the other from Nord's argument for more accommodation of religion in public-school curricula:

> Has anyone ever heard a pregame prayer? I have. Used to hear them all the time, in the '50s, at Corsicana High School football games. Guess what they prayed for over the P.A. system? America's conversion to the regimen of the First Methodist Church? Not a chance. Rather, for a clean game, and for the safe return of all fans to their homes. Gosh! What dangerous stuff! Likely to result in the overthrow of civilization! (Murchison, 2002, pp. 191–192)

> In the current culture wars, religious liberals tend to ally themselves with the educational establishment against those on the Religious Right who are attacking the public schools. In politics and theology, I line up with the left.

Nonetheless, I believe with the right that public education is hostile to religion—not least to liberal education. (Nord, 2002, p. 170)

Both examples are written in the first-person ("I"), but the first passage is much more informal, using colloquial, conversational expressions (e.g., "Gosh!") to make the writer's point. The attitude of this writer toward the issue at hand is sarcastic, particularly evident in his use of overstatement ("What dangerous stuff! Likely to result in the overthrow of civilization!"). The second example is more formal and serious, though it is equally direct and assertive.

So which is the more effective approach? That depends on the writer's rhetorical situation. The first writer, Bill Murchison, is a syndicated columnist, which means he probably has a following—that is, readers who read his column regularly. These readers probably read his column because they enjoy his writing style or because they tend to agree with his viewpoint on particular issues. They expect Murchison's writing to be informal and have an edge to it. With this audience his tone is probably effective. Warren Nord, on the other hand, is a university professor and is writing for a publication that examines issues of politics, culture, and theology. Readers of this kind of magazine expect more formal and serious commentary on these issues. Given each writer's rhetorical situation, each has adopted a tone that is appropriate and effective for his respective purpose and audience.

And this is the point: our rhetorical situations should dictate the mood or attitude we project in our writing. In a letter in which we try to persuade a friend to accompany us on a vacation, we can probably afford to use a casual, even playful tone; when writing a paper for our psychology teacher on cognitive development, however, casual and playful would likely prove an inappropriate rhetorical choice on our part.

Perhaps a real-life example will help make my point here. Several years ago my wife and I were vacationing in Hawaii. Returning from a dinner cruise, we discovered that the car we had been driving had been ticketed for parking with the rear of the car facing a parking meter. I had backed into the stall and put ample change into the meter for the time we would be away from the car. Needless to say, we were surprised that we had been ticketed. Neither of us had ever heard of an ordinance in any city that prohibits parking with the rear of the car facing a parking meter. Even my in-laws, who lived in Hawaii at the time, didn't know that parking in such fashion was illegal. It was only after contacting the traffic bureau that we learned that Honolulu has such an ordinance. What made matters worse, the fine was $100!

My initial reaction to the ticket was anger. I felt like, as a tourist, I had been taken advantage of. While there may have been good reason for the ordinance, I believed the city had an obligation to post signs on the meters informing drivers of the ordinance, especially since many drivers in Honolulu are tourists and are probably unaware of those laws unique to the city. Given the unusual nature of the ordinance, it seemed like a tourist trap, since I'm sure I wasn't the first tourist to be ticketed for this same infraction. And the $100 fine seemed excessive, to say the least.

I decided to fight the ticket. To do so, I would have to write a letter to the judge, since my vacation ended before I could appear in court. In planning my argument, I had to decide the tone I wanted my letter to take. As I've mentioned, I was angry at the time. Part of me wanted to unload on the judge in the most aggressive language I could muster. I realized, however, that this probably wouldn't be the most effective rhetorical approach. I assumed the judge probably wouldn't respond well to an angry or sarcastic assault on his city and its driving ordinances. If my goal was to persuade him to dismiss the fine, I decided I would need to make a calm and reasonable argument. But I also wanted to be assertive. Here is a passage from my letter:

> Given the relatively unusual nature of the ordinance as well as the number of tourists who visit Honolulu, I am surprised that signs explaining the ordinance are not posted in metered parking lots. It seems unreasonable to assume that visitors to your city and state would be aware of such an ordinance, nor is it likely that tourists are going to consult

the kinds of publications that explain those laws unique to Honolulu. It seems to me that your community has a responsibility to better inform visitors of the kinds of ordinances I unknowingly violated.

I'll let you determine how successful I was in creating a calm and reasonable tone. But just for fun, let's revise the passage so it reflects the way I felt at the time I received the ticket:

> Given the completely idiotic and senseless nature of the ordinance as well as the number of tourists who spend their hard-earned money in Honolulu, I can't believe that signs explaining this ridiculous ordinance aren't posted in metered lots. Do you really expect tourists, people on vacation, to take the time to read up on your driving ordinances? I would suggest that you and your city start doing a better job of informing people of your stupid laws.

While this second passage was fun to write, and perhaps more accurately expresses how I felt, it certainly wouldn't have been as rhetorically effective with my audience. (Incidentally, the judge eventually dismissed my ticket.)

One final thing. You will notice when comparing the two passages above that tone can be altered dramatically by only a word or two. Consider the different mood projected by referring to the ordinance as "idiotic" as compared to "unusual." Hence, whether creating tone or assessing someone else's tone, we need to pay particular attention to diction and recognize the options at our disposal. And we always need to be aware of the rhetorical situation and assess the effectiveness and appropriateness of tone in relationship to our subject, our purpose, and our audience.

CONCLUSION

Words ultimately make (or break) an argument. While we certainly need to attend to a variety of considerations when crafting an argument—rhetorical situation, our claims and use of evidence, etc.—we need to pay equal attention to each and every word we use, every figure of speech, and our tone. We need to realize that these features of our arguments go a long way in shaping the way our readers perceive us and the issues we address. We can have all the evidence in the world supporting our position, but if our language doesn't work, neither will the argument. And as individuals who are daily bombarded with one argument after another, we need to attune ourselves to the ways language works to produce an effect. We need to realize that the words others use to persuade us just aren't sending a message; they are working to influence and shape the way we look at the world.

In short, we need to be more conscious of language and its effects. As writers, we need to consider all of our options when deciding on the language we use to make our points. For example, when writing my letter to the judge regarding my parking ticket, I considered several words I could use to describe the parking ordinance I had violated—"idiotic," "stupid," "ridiculous," "odd," "unusual," etc. I chose "unusual" because it seemed like the least offensive and projected the tone I was aiming for. At another place in the letter, I thought an analogy might help me more effectively make a point: "Having and enforcing this ordinance on visitors [who are unaware of it] is like asking someone to play a game and not telling them the rules, and then penalizing them the second they break the rules." My goal in using the analogy was to describe what I perceived as the unjust nature of the law and its enforcement, and I thought a figure of speech might help my audience better understand how I felt at the time.

The point is that my word choice, my use of figurative language, and my tone were issues I thought through as I planned and executed my argument. I left nothing to chance, especially my language. As you decide on what evidence to use to support a claim, or what types of appeals will be most effective—ethical, emotional, logical—you likewise need to consider the linguistic issues we've explored in this chapter to effectively influence your audience.

When analyzing an argument, we should probably highlight words that seem especially significant and consider the implications of those words. In the passage describing the turtle-farming industry, the word "killer" is especially significant, so

I chose to focus on it and the associations we attach to it when analyzing the passage. We should also note when arguments are using figures of speech and flesh out all the implications of a figurative use of language. The allusions to crucifixion in the turtle passage come with a number of implications—the painful nature of the turtles' deaths, their status as the innocent victims of the brutality of others, etc. We likewise want to identify an author's tone and consider its appropriateness and effectiveness given the rhetorical situation. As when crafting an argument, we should attend to these details when presented with an argument. If we understand that words both reveal and shape our sense of reality, we cannot help but give language the attention it deserves.

REFERENCES

Batchelor, H. (Winter 1994). Sex education: Have we gone too far? In *115 in the Shade: A Journal of English 115 Student Writing* (pp. 31–32). Provo, UT: BYU English Department.

Gold, H. (2002). *The age of happy problems.* New Brunswick, NJ: Transaction.

Gorgias. (2001). *Encomium of Helen* (M. Gagarin & P. Wood, Trans.). In V. B. Leitch (Ed.), *The Norton anthology of theory and criticism* (pp. 30–33). New York: Norton.

Hemingway, E. (1957). *A farewell to arms.* New York: Collier.

Kerferd, G. B. (1981). *The sophistic movement.* Cambridge, England: Cambridge University Press.

LeMann, N. (2000, October 16 & 23). The word lab: The mad science behind what the candidates say. *The New Yorker,* 100–112.

Murchison, B. (2002). Restrictions on school prayer are unfair to students. In W. Dudley (Ed.), *Religion in America: Opposing Viewpoints Series* (pp. 189–192). San Diego, CA: Greenhaven Press.

Nord, W. A. (2002). Public schools should include more religion in the curriculum. In W. Dudley (Ed.), *Religion in America: Opposing Viewpoints Series* (pp. 169–177). San Diego, CA: Greenhaven Press.

Swan, R. (2002). Parents must provide necessary medical treatment for children regardless of religious belief. In W. Dudley (Ed.), *Religion in America: Opposing Viewpoints Series* (pp. 142–149). San Diego, CA: Greenhaven Press.

NOTES

NOTES

NOTES

Chapter

FINDING THE AVAILABLE MEANS

Inventing an Argument

Kristine Hansen

INTRODUCTION

When most of us hear the word *invention,* we are likely to think first of such things as the airplane, the computer, the polio vaccine, or other devices and processes that smart people have developed through persistent study and experimentation. We usually think of inventors as creative geniuses who defy tradition and conventional wisdom as they work all alone in their laboratories to bring forth their brain children. While we rightly celebrate inventors like Thomas Edison or the Wright brothers, we often forget that they also built on the work of others; what they created grew out of their insights into existing principles and ideas and their ability to make connections between those principles and ideas. They made a new contribution, to be sure, but it was possible to do so because some things were already available to them. In this chapter you are going to learn about the process of rhetorical invention, that is, the process of creating arguments that will persuade others. You are going to learn that rhetorical invention does not depend solely on genius and isn't necessarily the result of solitary effort made in lonely study. While individual effort is certainly necessary, rhetorical invention is very much rooted in shared understandings, values, habits of mind, and ways of using language.

The inventors of rhetoric, the ancient Greeks, and the people who further refined rhetoric, the ancient Romans, understood invention as the process of producing reasons, ideas, examples, stories, facts, comparisons, analogies, and other verbal matter for an argument. They certainly would have thought of an argument as a new creation, but they would have regarded it as persuasive to the extent that it grew out of existing ideas and principles already accepted. The Latin roots of the word *invent* may help you see why they thought this way: *in* meant "on," and *venire* meant "to come." So to invent substance for rhetoric was to come upon it or find it. A new argument could be generated by visiting the places (*topoi* or "topics") that helped a speaker or a writer find a starting point for a new argument when it was called for by a given purpose, situation, and audience (rhetorical situation). So important is invention in rhetoric that Aristotle famously defined rhetoric as the art of finding the available means of persuasion in any case whatsoever. His book *Rhetoric* is a comprehensive treatise that systematically lays out all that was known about the art of communication in Greece of the fifth century, and three-fourths of the book deals with invention alone.

THE FIVE "CANONS" OF RHETORIC

Invention is the first of the five "canons," or categories, of rhetoric. In effect, invention amounts to planning what you will say; it's all the work you do before you begin writing a draft. The second canon of rhetoric, **arrangement**, concerns organizing the invented matter in a sequence that will be clear and persuasive to the audience. The third canon of rhetoric, **style**, deals with putting the invented material in the best words and word order (syntax); it includes deciding whether to use such flourishes as repetition, parallelism, rhythm, alliteration, irony, metaphor, and other figures of speech. Although we usually associate these stylistic devices only with literary writing, they are also important in other kinds of rhetoric. Often style is thought of as mere ornament, but, as Burton (2003) reminds us, the root of *ornament* suggests the importance and centrality of style, for Latin *ornare* means "to equip, fit out, or supply." In other words, to use style well means to suit your language to your invented matter so that it will have maximum impact on your audience and accomplish your intentions. The fourth and fifth canons, **memory** and **delivery**, remind us that rhetoric was originally the art of speaking well. Once a rhetor had invented and arranged ideas, then fitted them out in the best words and in the most effective syntax, the next task was to commit the invented speech to memory and then to deliver it to the audience effectively. Now that rhetoric has become a focus of study in writing courses, little attention is paid to memory; even in speech courses, students seldom learn the elaborate methods of memorizing speeches that were taught in the past. But delivery still has an important analog in writing, as a carelessly edited and sloppily printed paper does not impress a reader any more than a speaker who mumbles, fidgets, and looks at the floor impresses a listener. This chapter addresses invention, Chapter 7 deals with arrangement, and Chapter 8 attends to style and delivery.

Nowadays, the names of the five canons of rhetoric are not generally used in textbooks about writing. Instead of invention, such books speak of planning, prewriting, or pre-drafting. Textbooks usually use the word organization instead of arrangement; they might also speak of typical patterns for different genres of writing, such as instructions or letters. While the term style is still used, the scope of what is treated under that heading is usually much narrower than in past centuries, often being limited to a treatment of rules of grammar, usage, punctuation, and mechanics. Instead of oral delivery, you are now more likely to be taught about document design so that the format of your writing will aid the reader's ability to understand. Even though the names of the parts of rhetoric have changed, it is clear that certain principles of clear communication have persisted through the centuries.

TWO APPROACHES TO INVENTION

Likewise, it is probably true to say that a persistent challenge for students, whether they lived in ancient Greece or Rome, during the European Renaissance, or in the twenty-first century, is to come up with smart things to say to impress the teacher and other readers. Do you find as you write an academic paper that the most time-consuming and agonizing part of the process is generating enough strong material to support your main claim and persuade your audience to accept it? Corbett (1965) states that a writer "must either *have* something to say or *find* something to say" (p. 94, emphasis in original). Sometimes students your age feel that they neither have enough to say nor know where to find more. That's why teachers over the centuries have tried two approaches to helping students be inventive in their rhetoric.

The first approach is to try to store students' minds with ideas and information the students can draw from later by having the students read books, listen to lectures, observe nature, and seek other experiences that will add to the knowledge they can turn to when they need to create an argument. The great Roman teacher Quintilian, for example, stressed giving young people a broad education in history, music, math, astronomy, and literature, so that when they were grown citizens they would be able to draw on their education to create rhetoric that would make their cities and nations better. Quintilian and many other teachers in past centuries helped students create this fund of knowledge by assigning imitation exercises in school; for example, the students would write prose paraphrases of poetry they read or verse paraphrases of prose passages, or they would write papers in which they drew a moral from a fable, from biography, or from a historical event that they retold. Then they would often memorize and recite what they had written. By practicing the language arts in this manner, students developed a copious store of information and a facility with words that helped them generate things to say when they faced novel rhetorical situations. The general education requirements that you fulfill at college grow out of this teaching tradition by exposing students to great ideas and moments in the history of our civilization. Hopefully, all that you are learning in your science, literature, history, and arts courses is creating a storehouse of knowledge in your mind that you can turn to when you need to invent matter for an argument. For example, the lessons you learn in a physical science class may come in handy as you craft an argument on the effects of global warming, or your history class's discussion of the Founding Fathers and the drafting of the Constitution may influence an argument on church-state separation.

The second approach teachers have tried—and this approach complements the first, so they are not mutually exclusive—is teaching students how to find an argument by giving them strategies and locations from which material can be generated. Like Quintilian, Cicero believed in giving students a broad education to prepare them to be good citizen-rhetors; but both Cicero and Aristotle also devised methods of helping students find or generate new matter for an argument. They outlined strategies called the "topics" and the "stases" for thinking systematically about the issue at hand. Both of these strategies will be discussed in this chapter along with research in the library and on the Internet as ways of finding the available means of persuasion for papers you are assigned to write.

COMMON TOPICS OF INVENTION

While you have the Internet at your fingertips to stimulate your thinking and help you locate facts and ideas when you are assigned a paper, students in the past had the topics. Today we think of a topic as something you write *about*, but in the past a **topic** (from Greek *topos*) was thought of as a *place* to find an argument. This meaning of topic is still preserved in words like *topical ointment*, a salve that you apply to an affected place on your skin, or *topographical map*, a map that tries to show the actual features of a landscape by giving the elevations within the area it represents. Perhaps the most famous lists of topics for invention come from Aristotle, who taught that all discourse could be divided into three categories: forensic or judicial speeches, deliberative or legislative speeches, and epideictic or ceremonial speeches. For each of these types of speeches, Aristotle listed special topics the speaker could go to in order to invent appropriate and persuasive things to say if he had to persuade a jury of his innocence, for example, or encourage fellow legislators to vote for a new law, or deliver the eulogy at a funeral.

But Aristotle also listed a number of common topics to stimulate invention for any kind of discourse, for any occasion, speaker, or audience. These topics are ways of thinking about an issue and are meant to help generate premises for making rhetorical arguments, such as Grant Boswell describes in Chapter 2. They are common not only because they are suited for any rhetorical situation but also because they represent shared habits of mind, values, and language use. Thus, they are effective starting points for building an argument because the audience is already disposed to accept the logic implicit in them. Students today can still use these topics as starting places for constructing arguments or as heuristics to guide their thinking. (The word *heuristic* comes from Greek *heuriskein,* meaning "to find.") Table 1 lists some of these common topics, using names and categories that various scholars have suggested from reading Aristotle and other theorists. Each topic is followed by an illustration of how it might be used to create an argument, either pro or con, about the issue of globalization. Note that you may not agree with some of these arguments, but that is beside the point. Each topic can be used to generate a number of arguments but doesn't guarantee their acceptance.

Table 1. Names and Illustrations of Some Common Topics

1.	Definition by class or category	Globalization is simply one more means of spreading democracy and freedom.
2.	Division of whole into parts	Globalization is a four-faceted phenomenon that affects nations economically, politically, culturally, and physically.
3.	Division into essence and accidents	Globalization is simply the spread of market economies throughout the world; everything else that changes in a country experiencing globalization is just a by-product.
4	Comparison by similarity	Globalization, like nineteenth-century imperialism, extracts the wealth from less-developed nations, leaving them poorer, while enriching powerful nations and corporations that have advanced technologies and great economic capital.
5.	Comparison by difference	Unlike nineteenth-century imperialism, globalization increases the wealth of every nation affected by it through expanding competition and making markets more efficient.

6.	Comparison by degree	Globalization differs from nineteenth-century colonization only in the fact that multinational corporations don't take over the governments of the nations they enter.
7.	Cause and effect	Third World nations that lowered tariffs and deregulated international business have lowered their poverty rates by accepting globalization.
8.	Antecedent and consequence	One consequence of globalization is increased urbanization, which brings more pollution to the planet, whose atmosphere is already warming from greenhouse gases.
9.	Contraries	Globalization is concentrating the world's wealth in the hands of a comparative few, so it must be promoting the poverty of all the rest.
10.	Contradictions	Outsourcing jobs either benefits the economy or it does not.
11.	Authority	According to the United Nations Human Development Report, globalization is creating new threats to human security.
12.	Testimonial	A young woman working in a U.S.-owned Nike factory in Thailand described how the workers were locked in the factory and permitted only one restroom break during an 8-hour workday.
13.	Statistics	Prof. Sala-i-Martin used 7 indexes to measure poverty around the globe, and he found there were between 300 and 500 million fewer poor people in 1998 than in the 1970s.
14.	Maxims	"A rising tide lifts all boats," so if global competition improves the standard of living of some people, eventually it will improve the standard of living for all.
15.	Precedents	The 40-year-old U.S. trade embargo on Cuba has failed to keep American products out of Cuba; attempts to regulate free trade elsewhere are likewise doomed to failure.

Some students might consider it artificial and cumbersome to refer to the above list of topics when considering an issue because their minds seem naturally to resort to thinking of ways to argue an issue from a definition or from authority. Other students, however, may find it very helpful—especially when they are stuck—to refer to this list of topics and see whether they can come up with a way of dividing the issue or of comparing it to something else, so they can invent a stronger argument. As noted in Chapter 2, you must consider your audience above all else and use the STAR principle as you plan the kinds of arguments that are likely to persuade your readers to accept the claim you want to make about an issue. For example, if you were writing a term paper arguing that globalization is good for the economies of Third World nations, your audience might accept the maxim "A rising tide lifts all boats" as relevant to your argument and possibly even accurate. But they likely would not find it a sufficient or typical argument to make about this issue. More likely, your audience would expect to see arguments that are grounded in authority, cause and effect, and statistics. So the particular topic or strategy of using a maxim to support your claim could only be a minor part of your invention process for such a paper.

THE STASES

Although the strategy of using the stases for invention was developed early in the history of rhetoric by the Greek Hermagoras, the Roman Cicero is usually given the credit for developing this idea fully, particularly to teach invention for judicial arguments. *Stases* is the plural of the word *stasis*, a Greek word that means "standstill." Thus, a **stasis** is a place on which an argument may stand or the point from which it can proceed. Table 2 gives the names of the four stases and questions to be asked about each.

Table 2: The Stases and Their Meanings

Fact	What is the issue? Does the issue exist? Is it true? Where did it come from? How did it begin? What is the cause? Can it be changed?
Definition	If the issue exists, what should it be called? How should it be defined? What kind is it? What are its parts and how are they related? To what class of things does the issue belong?
Quality	How serious or important is the issue? Is it good or bad, right or wrong, honorable or dishonorable?
Procedure	What should be done about the issue? What jurisdiction should take responsibility for the issue? What actions in regard to the issue are possible or desirable?

Using the stases to invent matter for an argument about an issue requires you to know your audience and their position with regard to the issue. Let's say you want to write a letter to one of the U.S. senators from your state asking him or her to introduce legislation intended to halt and even reverse global warming, a phenomenon that you think requires immediate action. But it would likely be pointless to tell the senator what kind of legislation you think should be introduced (a procedure) until you are sure that you and the senator both agree on the fact, the definition, and the quality of global warming. You need to find out which stasis or standpoint offers common ground for both you and the senator to start from in order to have a fruitful argument about this issue. So first you might look at the senator's website to see if there is any sort of position statement there about global warming; you could also look for news articles that would give you some idea of the senator's position on the issue. You would need to do this first because you want to find out whether the senator even considers global warming to be a **fact**. If you were to find a newspaper article stating that the senator considers all of the outcry about global warming to be just so much "science fiction," you would have to start at the first stasis because your immediate task would be to find arguments that persuade the senator that global warming is a fact.

But now suppose you find that the senator does agree that global warming exists; however, it is not a serious problem, just a temporary phenomenon that the planet undergoes from time to time. In that case, you would find the starting point for your argument at the second stasis, **definition**, and you would have to find arguments to persuade the senator to change his or her definition to match your definition of global warming as a human-caused phenomenon that might be reversible if the right actions are taken. Now suppose that the senator believed that global warming is a fact that should be defined as potentially catastrophic but that there is still plenty of time to deal with it. In that case, the point from which you would proceed is the third stasis, **quality**, because you would want to argue that the issue requires immediate action. Now suppose the senator agreed with you on the standpoint of quality; then it would be appropriate to move to the fourth stasis, **procedure**, and outline your argument for how to resolve the problem.

As you can see, using the stases as an invention strategy requires you to do a lot of background research about your audience so that you don't end up wasting your time arguing for what the audience already accepts or talking right past your audience because you haven't established the point at which you disagree. Using the stases as a heuristic narrows the scope of what you need to invent because you only need to make an argument about the stasis at issue. Debates in the United States about complex issues such as abortion or the role of religion in the public square are often not very fruitful because the people involved in these debates have not identified those parts of the issue they agree on, so they talk about everything at once. If they would proceed through the stases first, they could then focus on trying to persuade each other more systematically about the points where they disagree. The chances of reaching a consensus or a compromise are enhanced if the questions that are most urgently at issue are identified at the outset.

RESEARCH AS INVENTION

"The topics and the stases are all very fine and good," you might be saying at this point, "but what I have to write next is a research paper." If this is indeed your concern, you have identified an important means of invention all your professors will expect you to be able to use at college: library and Internet research. Inventing an argument through research is completely compatible with knowledge of the topics and stases because you will need to identify the type of information you find through your research in the library or on the Internet (you could do this with the topics) and decide the best way to use it in the argument you are constructing (you could do this with the stases). But before proceeding, we need to consider what a research-based issues paper requires you to do and what those requirements imply for the way you conduct your research.

The first requirement is that your research paper be an argument, not merely a compilation of what various authorities have said about an issue. This kind of paper may be new for you, as high school research papers often turn out to be mainly an exercise in finding and citing sources, and the main goal for many students is just to make the paper long enough. But the requirement of a research-based argument means that you must take a stand on a debatable issue. Rather than take a firm stand at the outset and then merely look for material to support it, it is best to approach your research with a sense of openness and questioning. So at first you should read your library and Internet sources to determine what stand you feel persuaded to take by those who have already thought and written about the issue. Going into your research with an open mind will be an advantage because you will be more likely to consider all sides of the issue carefully and thus take a position that is responsive to the complexities and nuances of the issue. In other words, you will be inventing your position as you read as well as inventing the substance of your paper by taking notes about all sides of the issue for later use.

Taking a well-informed and thoughtful position on the issue you choose will be important in creating a credible ethos and thus disposing your audience to give your argument careful scrutiny. Paying attention to your audience and to your ethos are second and third requirements of your research-based argument. Having your audience clearly in mind from the beginning will be an advantage as you begin the process of finding sources. You must not only choose sources that will be persuasive to your audience, but you must show that you have not overlooked sources that are not in accord with your position.

Your audience expects you to have arrived at your position on the issue after a careful and informed process of study. And if your audience is not inclined to agree with your position at the outset, they will particularly want to know why you have found counter-arguments unpersuasive. If you are to have credibility with your audience and gain a hearing for your claim, you must show that the reasons and evidence you offer for your claim are superior to those that could be advanced against your claim. As you can see, inventing your argument from the research you find will not be the work of a few hours—or even one long night of frantic reading and writing. The invention process for a research-based issues paper will need to extend over several days, if not weeks.

At this point it is important to note that rhetorical invention is not a completely explicable and tidy process. Although there are many aids to invention, such as the topics and stases, as well as various questions, checklists, and techniques explained in handbooks about writing, the best thing you can do as you are researching material for a paper is simply to allow yourself time to mull over the things you are reading and learning. Often, at the least expected times and places, you will have an "aha! moment" when something that you couldn't quite figure out suddenly becomes clear, or you see the way to resolve a contradiction, or the perfect illustration of a point comes to you. You simply must begin early enough to research, plan, and draft your paper so that you give yourself the maximum opportunity for these serendipitous moments to arise. Rather than thinking of your research as a distasteful chore to be gotten out of the way as quickly and painlessly as possible, think of it as a quest to discover the best information you can about an issue that is crucial to you and your audience; then think of your writing as the shaping of a compelling argument that will win the assent of your readers and even change their minds if necessary.

A (HYPOTHETICAL) CASE STUDY

To illustrate what I have been saying about inventing a claim and then an argument from research, let's consider a hypothetical case. A student, Sam, has decided to write his issue paper on prayer in public schools. At the beginning he thinks he knows what stand he wants to take: As a religious person who benefits from daily personal prayers, he believes that it would be a good thing for everyone to realize this benefit; and since most people go to public schools, if they learned there how to pray, he thinks they would be better off—and so would the entire nation as a result. So he begins his invention process thinking that eventually he will claim that prayer should be a daily part of the routine in public schools. But he is not sure this is the position he wants to take, so he begins his research with a willingness to change his mind as he reads and studies the various arguments that have already been made for and against prayer in public schools. He also begins his research with his audience in mind: the other members of his class. Sam knows that some of them are not religious at all and probably seldom or never pray, while others belong to various faiths, including Christians, Jews, Muslims, and Buddhists. Sam realizes that to invent a well-reasoned argument for this audience, he will have to be very thorough and thoughtful in his research.

The librarians at Sam's college have created background study guides in several general areas of interest to help first-year students follow a careful research process and avoid jumping to ill-founded conclusions. Sam downloads one on "Church and State in America," which directs him to read specialized encyclopedias, other reference works, and key articles that have already been identified as good background reading for this broad issue. As he reads, he begins to see that the issue is very complex and it has a long history. Intrigued all the more, he continues reading until he gets a sense of the extent of the debate and of the terminology that has been used to discuss it, such words as *prayer, religion, public education, schools*. Eventually, because his teacher requires it, Sam formulates two questions he will try to answer in his research: "Why have the courts ruled against requiring prayer in public school? Do these court rulings infringe on the free exercise of religion?" Now he is ready to locate sources that will give him material for answers to these questions.

Using the various terms he found in his background reading, Sam searches for books that deal with this issue. His first search of his library's catalog using the search terms "religion" and "public schools" returns 232 titles—too many! Narrowing his search to "prayer" and "public schools," Sam gets 52 titles— still too many to read. He decides to look at those books that have been published since 1990, on the assumption that they will sum up the history of the issue prior to that time and reflect the latest thinking on the issue. That still leaves 22 books, so Sam eliminates duplicates, a specialized book for attorneys, and one with very specific local reference. He now has 16 book titles, but he notes that three of them are currently checked out and won't be back in time to use before his paper is due. Going to the library, he finds the remaining 13 books. At this point, Sam reminds himself of the questions he is trying to answer: "Why have the courts ruled against requiring prayer in public school? Do these court rulings infringe on the free exercise of religion?" By looking at the table of contents and the index of each book, he is able to identify seven books that discuss court rulings on the issue and explain the judicial thinking behind the rulings. He notes that two of the books have an obvious bias, as one author states in the preface that she is an atheist, and another states in his preface that he is president of a group that is lobbying Congress to amend the Constitution to allow prayer in schools. But Sam figures it will be interesting to read what they have to say, so he checks these books out along with the others. As you can see, even though Sam has had to go through a rather lengthy process to get to the point where he can start reading about his issue in depth, it really only took about four hours. Sam's investment of time will pay off later, as he is not just grabbing any sources he can find, but selecting from all the ones available those that will help him invent an argument from the best current thinking about the issue.

Next Sam searches databases for periodical articles on the issue, using the search terms he identified. Once again, a daunting number of possible articles show up on the screen, but through a process of narrowing the search terms and winnowing out titles that are old, extreme, or not helpful, Sam comes up with a manageable number of articles. For some of these he can download the full text online; however, some he must look up in the periodicals of the college library. Before spending money on photocopies, Sam skims the articles, especially the abstract when available, to see if the article is one he wants to read thoroughly.

Armed with his books and articles, Sam now heads home. But that evening at home, he also decides to see what he can find on the Internet. Both his teacher and the librarians who created the background study guide have warned Sam that much information on the Internet is not reliable, so Sam turns first to Internet search engines recommended by his college library: INFOMINE, Internet Public Library, Librarians' Index to the Internet, Libraryspot, Refdesk.com, and Search Engine Showdown. He learned that these search engines will lead him to Web sites, electronic journals, and online documents that have been peer reviewed and deemed credible. At the end of his first day of research, Sam now has 7 books, 10 articles, and 5 web texts to work from—more than his teacher requires, but he can still eliminate those that are not helpful, redundant, or skewed. The available means of inventing his argument are now at hand.

Sam spends his research time the next few days reading and taking notes on his laptop computer. Soon he begins to see categories that he can sort his notes into, so he creates files for each category and saves his notes in the appropriate files. He is careful to put quotation marks around any words and sentences he copies directly from the source, along with page numbers and authors. Whenever he summarizes or paraphrases a source, he also writes the page numbers and authors. He knows he will have to document every borrowed idea in his paper, and he knows that nothing will undermine his credibility more than plagiarism. Sam wants his audience to be persuaded by his eventual argument, and he knows that part of the persuasion will come from how thorough and honest they perceive him to be.

As he continues to read and take notes, Sam finds his original position on school prayer shifting. Where he once favored making prayer a required part of the school day, he now begins to understand and accept the reasoning behind the court rulings that disallow required prayer. He learns that the First Amendment to the Constitution has consistently been interpreted to mean that the government cannot establish a preferred religion for the citizens of the country. Because public schools are run by the government, if they were to require students to participate in prayer, that would be like establishing a preferred religion, as it would be impossible to have a nondenominational prayer that satisfied the adherents of all possible religions—Christian, Jewish, Islamic, Buddhist, and so on—as well as those who do not adhere to any religion. Even allowing some students not to participate in the prayer wouldn't solve the dilemma because that would, in its way, still establish a religion by favoring believers over non-believers. To help make this point, Sam decides that he will quote from the U.S. Supreme Court ruling in *Santa Fe v. Doe* (2000): "School sponsorship of a religious message is impermissible because it sends the ancillary message to members of the audience who are non-adherents that they are outsiders, not full members of the political community, and an accompanying message to adherents that they are insiders, favored members of the political community." Sam has now found a position with respect to the first question he set out to answer: "Why have the courts ruled against requiring prayer in public school?"

But he still needs to answer his second question: "Do these court rulings infringe on the free exercise of religion?" At first it seemed to Sam that the answer was yes, because by not allowing prayer in school for those who would like to have it, the courts seem to prefer the interests of non-believers over those of believers. That in itself seems to be a way that the state "establishes" religion, i.e., by declaring it unimportant. But as Sam reads his sources, he learns that the courts have not ruled out *any* prayer in public school, but only *required* prayers led by teachers, who are employees of the government. Again and again, Sam reads that in the various court rulings, the judges have made clear that students can form groups that pray together at the school or study the Bible or any other religious book. It seems that students are able to freely exercise their religious beliefs while at school, but the school employees cannot require students to participate in religious observances. Sam decides that to help make this point he will quote from a 1998 directive from the U.S. Department of Education, which states the following:

Schools may not forbid students acting on their own from expressing their personal religious views or beliefs solely because they are of a religious nature. Schools may not discriminate against private religious expression by students, but must instead give students the same right to engage in religious activity and discussion as they have to engage in other comparable activity. Generally, this means that students may pray in a nondisruptive manner during the school day when they are not engaged in school activities and instruction, subject to the same rules of order that apply to other student speech. (Riley, 1998)

So after about 12 hours of reading and note-taking, Sam is now prepared to craft a claim about this issue that he will use as the thesis of his argument: "The courts have ruled correctly that public schools may not require students to participate in prayers as part of the curriculum because such a requirement would amount to violating the constitutional ban on a state-established religion. However, the courts have also ruled correctly that students may voluntarily participate in extracurricular prayer on school premises because to forbid them from doing so would violate their constitutional right to the free exercise of religion. In both cases, the court has made clear that the position of the school with respect to religion must be one of neutrality." Sam realizes that he may change this statement of his thesis as he drafts and revises his paper, but for now he has a claim that is more informed and more nuanced than his original position. And it is one that he can defend well in his paper for the audience that will read his paper. Even though he is a religious person who values prayer, Sam doesn't feel that he is being untrue to his principles by taking this stand. From his research, he has come to realize that he lives in a society with all kinds of religions and all degrees of adherence to the teachings of those religions. Thus, he has come to view the court rulings as the best possible solution to an issue that could be terribly divisive in a pluralist society. Sam feels confident that he can now explain this position to an audience and support it with the best available evidence.

CONCLUSION:
JOINING THE CONVERSATION

Sam's story illustrates how doing research is both a process of finding the available material to support your position *and* a process of establishing the position you will take. There is an interplay between these two processes that you should welcome as you immerse yourself in finding and reading the best sources you can locate. In these sources you will find reasons, analogies, facts, statistics, authorities, testimonials, precedents, anecdotes, causes, effects, and a number of other means of persuasion that you can use in your argument—in short, you will find material that can be classified using the common topics of invention and applied to whatever stasis is relevant for the audience you are addressing. By finding these materials and weaving them together to make your own argument, you enter the grand conversation about the important issues that face us, a conversation that sustains both scholarly and civic life. This conversation was described in the following way by a twentieth-century rhetorician named Kenneth Burke:

> Imagine that you enter a parlor. You come late. When you arrive, others have long preceded you, and they are engaged in a heated discussion, a discussion too heated for them to pause and tell you exactly what it is about. In fact, the discussion had already begun long before any of them got there, so that no one present is qualified to retrace for you all the steps that had gone before. You listen for a while, until you decide that you have caught the tenor of the argument; then you put in your oar. (pp. 110–111)

Strong rhetorical invention gives you the means to "put in your oar"—to take a turn in the conversation even though you are only a young college student and others older and wiser than you seem to have already said everything that could be said. Even though a lot has already been said, no one will have made the argument quite like you can. The continuation of society depends on this conversation continuing, so you must take your turn, even though you may think you are too young and inexperienced to do so. As you grow older, it will be even more important for you to participate in this conversation as a citizen of this nation and of the world, and it will be critical for you to help teach the next generation how a democracy sustains itself through argument. The course you are now taking in writing and argumentation is not just a hoop you jump through so you can get a diploma; it will be the foundation of your college education and your preparation for civic life. You have an academic and a civic responsibility to know what others have said about the issues that face us, to use the available means of invention to define and establish your own positions, and to make them as persuasive as possible so that you can influence the course of the society you live in.

REFERENCES

Burke, K. (1941). *The philosophy of literary form.* Berkeley: University of California Press.

Burton, G. (2003). Style. *Silva rhetoricae: The forest of rhetoric.* Retrieved May 25, 2006, from http://humanities.byu.edu/rhetoric/silva.htm

Corbett, E. (1965). *Classical rhetoric for the modern student.* New York: Oxford University Press.

Riley, R. (1998). *Secretary's statement on religious expression.* Retrieved May 25, 2006, from http://www.ed.gov/Speeches/08-1995/religion.html

Santa Fe Independent School District v. Doe, 530 U.S. 290, 390 (2000).

NOTES

NOTES

NOTES

Chapter

ARRANGING AN ARGUMENT

Form and Function

Grant M. Boswell

INTRODUCTION

By now you know something about arguments and invention in the rhetorical tradition of argumentation. Following invention, the second canon of the rhetorical tradition is arrangement or judgment. A canon in its original sense is a standard for measuring, but we use the term now in the sense of a rule or guiding principle. Both arrangement and judgment treat the ways to lay out an argument for the reader, but the guiding principle is form.

What do we mean by **form**? This is a difficult question, but I would like to approach it in terms of how readers respond to what they read. Let me start with a question that I hope will allow us to get at a working definition of form. Try to remember when you were young and one of your parents or a sibling or a teacher read a book to you. If you were like many small children, you liked to hear the same story over and over again. In fact, you probably had your favorite bedtime story memorized. If your mother or father read it to you and slipped up, you would correct them, or if you were really obsessive, you might make them start over. Why did you do that? Why do children like to hear the same story over and over again and insist that the reader get it right?

Now think of a book or a movie or a song that you like. How many times have you read it, seen it, heard it? Why do you keep reading, watching, listening to it? Nothing really changes. The hero in the book or movie doesn't get killed the thirteenth time through; the unrequited love of the forlorn vocalist isn't magically rewarded if you keep replaying the song. Why do we keep reading the same books, watching the same movies, listening to the same songs when the outcome doesn't change? Because we get a great deal of satisfaction in seeing things unfold as we have come to expect. That is the power and the pleasure of form.

As writers we might learn something by considering the power of form. Form keeps readers reading to make sure their formal expectations are met. To employ a powerful tool such as form, however, places some heavy obligations on us as writers. We wouldn't want to violate our readers' sense of form by not meeting their expectations. That might have disastrous consequences for us as writers.

READERS READING

To understand what those disastrous consequences might be, let's consider your habits as a reader. What do you read when you don't have to read for school? Newspapers? News magazines? Trade magazines? Novels? Biographies? Science fiction? Let's say that you are reading the paper. How do you read it? Do you start with the headlines? The comics? The sports page? The society page? Business? My grandmother used to go straight to the obituaries because she wanted to see if anyone she knew had died recently. We all read what we find interesting, entertaining, enjoyable, or relevant. Suppose you are in the market for a used car. On a normal day you might pick up the paper and go straight for the crossword puzzle, but today you go to the classified ads to look for a deal on a car. That is, a particular interest can take priority over something you usually enjoy. We all read what we find enjoyable, but sometimes what is interesting and relevant can take precedence.

Now ask yourself what you do when you read an article in a magazine or in a newspaper and you get to the bottom of the page and find that the article is continued on page 139 or in section B. Do you take the trouble to find the rest of the article and read it? You do only if you are really interested in it. Most of the time you probably say, "Oh well, it isn't that interesting," and you move on to another article or section of the paper. This is the way we generally read. We read what we are interested in, and when it ceases to be interesting or is too much trouble, we stop and go on to something else.

As writers we need to remember that our readers are just like we are: they won't keep reading unless they are kept reading by something they find interesting, enjoyable, or relevant. As writers we need to remember that real readers, unlike teachers, don't have to read to the end. It would be disastrous for us as writers to write an argument and have our reader stop reading midway through the second page. We would have lost the opportunity to present our case in its entirety; we would have lost the opportunity to influence our reader. But as writers we now know that form is a very useful and powerful tool to keep readers reading. Clearly, we need to know more about form and how it works.

DEFINING FORM

I like Kenneth Burke's definition of form. Burke was one of the great rhetoricians of the twentieth century and his definition of form is right on: "Form in literature is an arousing and fulfilling of desires. A work has form in so far as one part of it leads a reader to anticipate another part, to be gratified by the sequence" (1968, p. 124). Although Burke is talking about form in literature, form works the same way in nearly everything else you can think of. Think of every sit-com you've ever seen. Some situation is disrupted by an event and, as a viewer, you feel compelled to see how the situation is resolved. This is the basic pattern: scene, disturbance, resolution. It is also the basic form of most novels, stories, jokes, movies, and songs. Some kind of expectation is created and you feel compelled to see the expectation fulfilled.

When the fulfillment is unsatisfactory, you feel cheated. Have you ever seen a movie that ends in a way you didn't expect or in which the plot isn't fully resolved? Sometimes such endings can be a pleasant surprise, but other times you leave the theater disappointed. What you were longing for was for your expectations to be fulfilled and they weren't. It is a very unsatisfying feeling. But that is the power of form. We want to see our desires fulfilled; we want our expectations met; we want to see problems solved; we want to have doubts resolved; we want our questions answered. And we will stick around until they are fulfilled, met, solved, resolved, or answered.

There is a good story about the power of form I like to tell my students. I heard it once and don't know if it is true, but it is a good story. The child prodigy Mozart was like most other children in that he didn't like to get up in the mornings. His mother learned that if she played a chord sequence and left it unresolved, Mozart would have to get up and resolve it. But then he was up. I hope it is true because it illustrates the power of form so well.

So now we know that form has strong appeal for us. It kept us listening to our bedtime stories to make sure they were read to us just as we had come to expect. It keeps us watching the same movies, listening to the same songs, reading the same books for the very same reason. It keeps us watching, listening to, or reading something to see how our expectations will be fulfilled even when we may not be all that interested. So how does this knowledge help us as writers?

THE PARAGRAPH AND FORM

Let's talk about form at the paragraph level first. Once we have learned how form works in paragraphs, we can extrapolate and apply the same principle to an entire paper. You probably know that every paragraph needs to have a point. On reading comprehension tests you may have been taught to look for the sentence that states the point of the paragraph. Sometime this is called the topic sentence. As writers you probably have been taught to include topic sentences in your paragraphs. It turns out that this is very good advice. Why? Because readers expect paragraphs to have points.

We just learned that whenever readers, viewers, or listeners have expectations, those expectations need to be met, or the readers, viewers, and listeners will feel cheated. And now we know why they feel cheated: their formal expectations have not been met. So paragraphs must have points or readers feel cheated. This is very useful information for writers. The last thing you as a writer want to do is make your reader feel cheated. So where does the point of a paragraph have to occur? Where do readers expect the point of the paragraph to be? We need to know the answer to this question so we can meet our readers' expectations for form at the paragraph level. Readers expect the point of the paragraph to be in one of two places: at the beginning or at the end. Either place will do, but putting the point in the middle of the paragraph will not do because that is not where readers expect it. Let's take the most common case in paragraphs: the point-first paragraph.

POINT-FIRST PARAGRAPHS

Most of the paragraphs you read are **point-first paragraphs**. The point of the paragraph, the sentence that sums everything up or that states the main idea in its most general form, usually comes at the beginning of the paragraph. The rest of the sentences in the paragraph amplify, qualify, illustrate, or specify the point, adding information, comparing or contrasting, or increasing the level of specificity. That is the way most paragraphs work in English.

Take, for example, the paragraph you just read. The point of the paragraph is the first sentence: "Most of the paragraphs you read are point-first paragraphs." The second sentence amplifies this point by repetition. The third sentence adds additional information. The fourth sentence adds information about how paragraphs function and provides closure. That's it. That is how most paragraphs in English work. The formal expectation is created by stating the point in the first or second sentence (in a long paragraph possibly even the third sentence) and adding information to the point. As long as the point occurs early in the paragraph and as long as the rest of the sentences are relevant to the point, the readers' expectations are fulfilled and the paragraph is well formed. In point-first paragraphs the point serves two functions: it creates the expectation for what is to follow, and it states the point.

POINT-LAST PARAGRAPHS

I mentioned, however, that not all paragraphs are point-first paragraphs. And since we know that the point can't occur in the middle because readers don't expect it there, the only other option is for the point to occur at the end. These paragraphs are called **point-last paragraphs**, and although they are not as common as point-first paragraphs, they can teach us something very important about form.

Let's take a look at the paragraph you just read. What's the point? I think the point is the last sentence: "These paragraphs are called **point-last paragraphs**, and although they are not as common as point-first paragraphs, they can teach us something very important about form." But if it's a point-last paragraph how is it well formed? In the point-first paragraph we noticed that the point served two functions: first to create an expectation, second to state the point. In a point-last paragraph the point is obviously stated at the end, so what creates the expectation? In the paragraph above the first sentence does: "I mentioned, however, that not all paragraphs are point-first paragraphs." The first sentence signals that there is an exception to what we learned earlier. The "however" tells you that a contrast is coming, so you expect one. That expectation is met when you learn that point-last paragraphs can teach us something very important about form.

So, what do point-last paragraphs teach us about form? We know that form is the creation and fulfillment of an expectation. And we know that in a point-last paragraph the point— that is, the fulfillment—is at the end. So there has to be something at the beginning to create the expectation. Point-first paragraphs do the same thing, only the topic sentence has to do double duty: it has to both create the expectation and state the point. A point-last paragraph, however, teaches us that the creation of an expectation and its fulfillment can be separated for effect, and this two-fold sense of form is the one that many arguments employ, and there is a good reason for this.

MANAGING INFORMATION

The point-last model of form at the paragraph level will be important later, so I want you to remember it, but right now we need to learn something else about form at the paragraph level that will also be useful when we talk about the form of an entire argument. We know that paragraphs have to have a point, but there is something else that paragraphs have to do to be formally complete: paragraphs have to manage information according to reader expectations. So we need to know what we mean by "information" and what reader expectations are for managing information at the paragraph level.

Information comes in two flavors: old and new. **Old information** is information you can assume that your readers already know from general knowledge or information that you have already mentioned. Once you mention a bit of information it becomes old information. **New information** is information that you can't assume your readers already know or information that you haven't already mentioned. That's easy enough, but what expectation do readers have for how old and new information is managed?

It so happens that English-speaking readers have very definite expectations of how they want their information managed. Readers expect old information to be placed at the beginning of sentences and new information after the main verb. So a good sentence should manage information by placing information that your readers already know or that you have already mentioned at the beginning of the sentence, usually in the subject. New information, the stuff your readers may not know or that you haven't mentioned yet, goes after the verb or in the predicate. So the information flow of English sentences is old to new. Let's take a look at the sentence you just read. The subject is "information flow." I have already mentioned information and its management, so "information flow" can reasonably be assumed to be old information. The verb is "is," and the predicate is the verb plus the rest of the sentence. So the new information is "is old to new." This description of the relation of old and new information is something I have not mentioned before, so it is new information and is appropriately placed in the predicate.

But this is management of information at the sentence level. What do readers expect of information managed at the paragraph level? Readers expect that the old information in a paragraph will be fairly consistent. That is, if you underline all the subjects in the main clauses of the sentences in a paragraph, you should see that there is some consistency in the underlined words. Let's look at a paragraph I wrote earlier to see how I did at managing old and new information. I am going to underline the subjects of the main clauses to see if they form a relatively consistent string of old information.

> I like Kenneth Burke's definition of form. Burke was one of the great rhetoricians of the twentieth century and his definition of form is right on: "Form in literature is an arousing and fulfilling of desires. A work has form in so far as one part of it leads a reader to anticipate another part, to be gratified by the sequence" (1968, p. 124). Although Burke is talking about form in literature, form works the same way in nearly everything else you can think of. Think of every sit-com you've ever seen. Some situation is disrupted by an event and, as a viewer, you feel compelled to see how the situation is resolved. This is the basic pattern: scene, disturbance, resolution. It is also the basic form of most novels, stories, jokes, movies, and songs. Some kind of expectation is created and you feel compelled to see the expectation fulfilled.

I am going to list the words I have underlined and then describe whether the word is old information or not.

I	"I" (writer) known (old info)
Burke	mentioned in previous sentence (old info)
his definition of form	already mentioned (old info)
form	mentioned (old info)
Some situation	not mentioned (new info—oops!)
This	refers to preceding concept (old, but vague)
It	refers to pattern mentioned (old info)
Some kind of expectation	mentioned previously (old info)

This is a very helpful exercise for two reasons. First, it tells me if I have managed old and new information according to reader expectations. If we look at the list of words, we can see a string of old information that centers around "Burke's definition of form." So I didn't do too badly. When we manage old information consistently in paragraphs, we produce what is called **co-hesion**. This paragraph is fairly cohesive because the old information is managed fairly consistently. The consistency of old information gives the reader the sense that we are on topic. But the second reason this process is useful is that I can make the paragraph more cohesive by revising. I can revise the sentence beginning with "Some situation . . ." by adding a phrase: "In sit-coms some situation. . . ." This addition ties the sentence a little better to the previous quote from Burke that discusses form in literature. And I can revise the sentence beginning with "This" to read "This sequence," referring to the sequence already mentioned of situation, disturbance, and resolution. This revision would make the old information more explicit and, therefore, improves the cohesion. I recommend checking for cohesion as a revision strategy. If you ever get a comment in the margin such as "I can't make sense of this paragraph" or "I'm having a hard time following you here," chances are the paragraph is incohesive because you have not managed information according to reader expectations.

To sum up, for a paragraph to be well formed it has to have a point. The point usually occurs at the beginning, but it can also occur at the end. If the point occurs at the end, the paragraph has to have a sentence at the beginning that creates an expectation in the reader as to what the point might be. And finally, the paragraph has to manage information on the sentence level from old to new and produce cohesive strings of old information among the sentences.

FORM AND THE ARGUMENT

Now that we know how form works at the paragraph level, we can make the jump to hyperspace and see how the same principle of form works at the discourse level, or at the level of the paper. We have two models for form. Let's talk about the merits of each. The first is when the opening statement has to perform the two functions of creating the expectation and stating the point. If we use this model, we are talking about something you are already familiar with. It is the use of the thesis statement at the beginning of your paper. The thesis statement usually tells your reader what the point of your essay will be. Moreover, the thesis statement does create an expectation, although a minimal one. The only real expectation that a traditional thesis statement creates in your reader is whether you provide the evidence to support the point that you have already announced. This is not much of an expectation, but there are some genres of writing in which this is the preferred way of establishing the formal parameters of your paper.

Many proposals are written in this way. Whoever is going to evaluate the proposal wants to know up front what the proposal is in order to evaluate the rest of the evidence in light of the proposal. Much academic writing falls into this same mode of reading. The teacher wants to know up front what your point is in order to evaluate the rest of the essay in light of the point you have already announced. The teacher then grades you on how well you did what you said you were going to do. A thesis statement that both announces the point of the essay and creates an expectation, albeit a minimal expectation, is often found in writing that has to be evaluated for approval or for a grade. And since most of the writing you are doing at the university is academic writing, you would be well advised to follow the traditional thesis-first model. You may want to discuss this with your writing teacher to see if he or she has a preference. The important points for you to remember are these. First, you must create some expectation in order to set the formal expectations for your paper. Second, you must meet your readers' expectations. If your teacher expects a thesis-first approach, then by all means meet that expectation. To do otherwise might jeopardize your grade.

For some rhetorical situations, however, the traditional thesis statement at the beginning of the essay that announces the point of your essay is not always a good idea. Why not? Remember that we defined the claim in Chapter 2 as initially unacceptable to your reader. What do you think would happen if you announced to a real reader a thesis or a claim that was initially unacceptable? Readers don't read anything they don't find interesting or relevant. If you were to announce a thesis that your reader finds unacceptable, the reader is likely to do one of two things. The reader might simply dismiss the paper because of the unacceptable claim and move on to that re-run on TV, or the reader might go ahead and read the argument, but do so with a resistant attitude. Either way your chances of making an argument that actually influences the reader are diminished. So, what I am telling you is that the traditional thesis statement, although useful for some genres of writing, is not always the best choice in an argumentative essay. So if you don't put a thesis statement that announces your point at the beginning of the essay, what do you do?

The principle of the thesis statement is sound in that an expectation has to be made to create a sense of form for your reader. The announcement of an initially unacceptable point, however, will probably work against you in an argument. But remember what we learned from the point-last paragraph? You can make your point, that is, arrive at your claim at the end of your essay, but you still have to create an expectation for your reader at the beginning without tipping your hand. We mentioned earlier that form is created by creating an expectation, by posing a problem, by making a promise, or by asking a question. These are all good strategies for setting the formal constraints of your paper for two reasons: first, they have the advantage of creating a much stronger expectation for your reader than merely announcing what you plan to do. Asking a good question can keep the reader reading. Second, a good question has the advantage of not telling your reader what your claim is, a claim the reader is likely to object to right off the bat. So the model of form from the point-last paragraph is a much better model for setting the formal constraints of an argument when addressing a potentially hostile audience because it creates a genuine expectation in your reader and it does not put your reader off.

So now we know that a question is a good way to create an expectation and set the formal parameters of an argument. Where are we going to find a good question? Remember from Chapter 2 that we already discussed how arguments arise from

questions at issue. If you have done your argumentative analysis and know what is at issue for your reader, then you already have a good question. You can, in fact, use your issue question to create an expectation for your reader. Typically, the question would be posed to your reader at the end of your introduction. In creating a strong expectation for our reader by posing the question at issue, you are setting the formal constraints of your paper by the parameters set forth in the issue question. I say constraints because you are constraining the reader and you are constraining yourself to those parameters.

THE READER/WRITER CONTRACT

We call the use of the issue question, or some other means, to create a strong expectation in your reader the **reader/writer contract**. Like all contracts, the reader/writer contract binds both parties. The reader promises implicitly to keep reading so long as the writer addresses the question at issue. If the writer ever strays and becomes irrelevant, gets off topic, or writes in a way the reader doesn't perceive as addressing the question, the reader is justified in stopping reading. I know this may sound harsh, but one of the most useful comments a teacher can make on a student paper is this: "If I didn't have to read this paper, I would stop right here because I can't see how this paragraph relates to the question you posed in your introduction."

The reader/writer contract obligates both reader and writer— the reader to keep reading, the writer to be relevant to the question at issue. If the reader ceases reading, he or she can be accused of not giving the argument a fair shot and of being closed-minded. If the writer gets off topic, he or she has broken the contract and the reader can justifiably stop reading and move on to something else. A broken contract is a serious problem for the writer of an argument because he or she gives up the opportunity to present the best case and loses the opportunity to address the reader on an issue of mutual importance.

A writer then must set the formal constraints of the argument by making a reader/writer contract. The contract can be made by using the issue question, but it must be something that keeps the reader reading and does not put the reader off by announcing the point or the claim of the argument. In this way form at the essay level works very similarly to form at the paragraph level. But the similarity between the essay and the paragraph does not stop at creating an expectation to keep the reader reading and to keep the writer on topic.

MANAGING OLD AND NEW CONCEPTS

In fact, we can manage information at the essay level according to the same principle that we learned by making paragraphs cohesive. We can discuss old information first and move from old to new information. To avoid confusion, we probably should not talk about "information" at the level of the essay because we are really dealing with concepts in an argument rather than bits of information in a paragraph. But the principle is sound. We can begin our argument with an "old" concept, a concept familiar to our reader. How do we know what is familiar to our reader?

We can return to our issue question. We learned in Chapter 2 that a question at issue generates the conditions for arguments. We can reasonably assume that if we have analyzed the situation carefully and have discovered the question that seems to be at issue for those who are making arguments, then we know what the issue question is. But more than that, we also know that the issue question poses a potential relationship between concepts. Let's retrieve an issue question that we examined in Chapter 2 to see how this might work:

> What consequence does making illegal immigration a felony have on the security of our borders?

We examined this question and found that it asserts a relation between two concepts: making illegal immigration a felony [concept A] and the security of our borders [concept B]. Since both concepts make up the question at issue and the issue is important to our reader, we can assume that both concepts are familiar to our reader. So in beginning an argument you would want to write an introduction. A good historical narrative that gives the history of the problem and frames the current issue would work well. Or you could try a "some say this, some say that" introduction in which you summarize the position of those who favor making illegal immigration a felony and those who do not. Or there are several other possible ways of writing an introduction. Once you have written your introduction, you then make a reader/writer contract. We can use our issue question as our contract.

Now we are ready to launch our argument. Let's begin with concept B, the security of our borders. We can talk about all kinds of things with respect to our borders: their length; the remoteness of long stretches of the borders; the difficulty of patrolling long, remote borders; the agencies charged with the responsibility of patrolling the borders; the number of border-patrol workers; technology now employed to patrol the borders; technology being planned or developed for patrolling the borders; citizen-volunteer efforts to patrol the borders; security risks, both real and imagined, of a porous border. As you can see, we have a lot to talk about in discussing concept B.

Or we could start with concept A. We could discuss the proposal to make illegal immigration a felony. Who proposed it? Where? What is the current penalty for illegal immigration? How many illegal immigrants now reside in this country? How many are estimated to enter each year? What measures have been taken in the past? Did they work? We have just as much to talk about with concept A as we did with concept B, and either discussion would be a reasonable place to start because both concepts would be familiar to our reader (old information).

How we go about structuring the rest of the argument will require that we return to the entire argument that we developed in Chapter 2. The argument, as you may recall, consists of a claim that answers the issue question, a reason, and an assumption. In developing the entire argument, you must know what the parts of the argument are in order to lay them out in a reasonable sequence for your reader. Here's one version of the argument we came up with in Chapter 2:

> Making illegal immigration a felony <u>decreases</u> the security of our borders because, as long as the US economy creates the "pull effect," the potential deterrence of the felony

charge <u>will encourage</u> illegal immigrants to develop more sophisticated and daring means to enter our country.

We have already decided that after an introduction in which we make a reader/writer contract, we need to start with a concept already familiar to our reader. Since the claim consists of two concepts from our issue question, we can begin with either of them because both should be familiar to our reader. If you have done the conceptual work well in asking a good issue question, answering it with specific attention to your audience, providing a reason that meets the STAR criteria (see Chapter 2), and checking your assumption to insure that it is acceptable to your intended audience, then you should be able to proceed through your argument in a way that makes sense to you and to your reader.

DISPOSING THE ARGUMENT

There are, however, a few guidelines that you will want to follow in laying out your argument. The technical term for laying out the argument is **disposition**. So, here are the guidelines for disposing the argument. Start with a concept familiar to your audience. Then move to another concept. You must discuss concepts before you relate them. Save the relationship between concepts for last because it is your claim and therefore your conclusion.

Just to make sure we all know what I am talking about, let's review all the parts and relations of the argument on illegal immigration. I will then lay out one possible disposition of the argument. Remember that in the claim we have concept A ("making illegal immigration a felony") and concept B ("the security of our borders"). They are related in the claim by the verb "decreases." Our reason with its parts labeled looks like this: "because, as long as the US economy creates the 'pull effect' [qualifier], the potential deterrence of the felony charge [repetition of concept A] <u>will encourage</u> illegal immigrants to develop more sophisticated and daring means to enter our country [concept C]." It is essential that the first concept of the reason be a repetition of concept A in the claim. The repetition of concept A in the reason provides the "lynch pin" that holds the argument together, since the question at issue centers on the consequences of making illegal immigration a felony. (Just to keep track of concept A, I have distinguished it in the reason by labeling it as A prime [A'].) Along with the reason, we can't forget the procatalepsis, or the anticipation of the reader's "buts." Last of all we know from Chapter 2 that there is an assumption that underlies the claim and reason. Below I will dispose the argument in an outline, estimating how many paragraphs I might write on each part and relation.

Introduction plus contract	Historical narrative	2 ¶'s
Concept B	Security of borders	2 ¶'s
Concept A	Proposal to felonize	1 ¶
Concept A'	Intent to deter by felonizing	1 ¶
Concept C	Sophisticated, daring means	2 ¶'s
Qualifier	The "pull effect"	1 ¶
A' will encourage C	Reason(s) meeting STAR criteria	2 ¶'s
Procatalepsis	Raise and meet objections	1 ¶
Whatever will encourage C also decreases B	Assumption as common ground	1 ¶
Therefore A decreases B	Conclusion	1 ¶
Disposition	Argument	14 ¶'s

I have tried to be conservative in estimating the number of paragraphs it would take to discuss the concepts and relations. As we saw above, there is a lot to say about each concept and, if you have done some research, a lot to say about your reason and procatalepsis. If you write about three paragraphs per page, the disposition schematized above is a four-page paper. If you expand the discussion of the concepts and relations, it can be much longer. The nice thing about disposing an argument as we have is that you can expand or contract it as needed. The basic argument can easily be done in three to four pages with a relatively basic discussion of concepts and relations. With some research and preparation, you can expand the argument into a much longer paper.

I want to emphasize that the scheme I outlined above is just one possible disposition of the argument. We could have just as easily started with Concept A, moved to A', then to C, then to the reason and procatalepsis, then to Concept B, then to the assumption, and finally to the conclusion. All you need to do is follow the guidelines for disposing an argument, and they are fairly simple: begin with an introduction and contract; start the argument with either Concept A or Concept B; discuss the other concepts of the argument before you relate them; save the relationship between Concept A and Concept B for last because it is your conclusion.

DISPOSITION AND PERSUASION

Now we know how to dispose an argument, but we may want to know how the disposition of an argument contributes to the overall persuasive force of the argument. We already learned that readers expect an essay to be well formed and that form has a very compelling effect on readers to keep reading. If we set up the argument with a reader/writer contract and make sure our argument sticks to the expectation we have created, then we will have met our readers' formal expectations. Moreover, in meeting our readers' expectations for form, we will also be assuring our readers that we have their best interest at heart. After all, we are meeting their formal expectations.

Readers also have expectations for reasonableness (logos). That is, our readers expect us to dispose the argument in a way that they can follow. If we have done our conceptual work well and have disposed the argument following the guidelines we learned, the readers should be able to follow the argument without too much trouble. The function then of the formal appeal and a good disposition is to take the readers through a rational process that the readers have not traveled on their own. It is as if we are guides and our readers want to see something we find beautiful, but they have never hiked this path before. With some help they can hike the path and see what we want to show them. Hopefully, they find the journey as worthwhile as we do, but the point is that they would not have taken it on their own. They need a guide, and as their guide we want the journey to be as easy and straightforward as we can make it.

In addition to leading our readers through the reasoning, a good disposition of the argument will have the additional effect of increasing the readers' confidence in us as writers (ethos). Our readers will believe that we are sensible and fair, that we share their interests, and that they can trust us as their guides. I don't know if you have ever had the experience of arriving in an unfamiliar city and hailing a taxi. You get in and hope that the driver knows where he's going and will get you there as fast and directly as he can. You are never sure, but you hope the driver is not running up the meter by taking a circuitous route. Still, you are a bit nervous. You don't want your readers to be nervous. You don't want your readers to feel like you are taking them on an aimless ride. By making and keeping your contract with your reader and by disposing the argument in a reasonable and clear manner, you assure your readers that you can be trusted and that your reader is in good hands. Thus, disposition enhances the persuasive force of an argument because it increases the ethical appeal that you as a writer have.

But that's not all disposing the argument well does. A good disposition of the argument also affects your readers (pathos). A well-disposed argument has a certain force or trajectory or momentum all its own. If the momentum of the argument is established by its disposition, at some point the reader ceases to worry about you the writer and starts to enjoy the argumentative force itself. The reader starts to go along for the ride and take pleasure in its movement. You may have had the experience of going on a ride at an amusement park. At first you are nervous, but after a while you stop worrying and start to enjoy the ride. A well-disposed argument can have this same effect on the reader. The reader gains confidence in the argument itself and enjoys the argumentative momentum. Thus, a well-disposed argument has an effect on the reader's attitude not just toward you, the writer, but also toward the argument itself. The reader begins to have confidence in the argument.

A well-disposed argument increases the reader's confidence in you the writer and in the argument itself to be sure, but that's not all. It has one other effect on the reader. If you can establish a momentum or trajectory in your argument, and if the reader begins to have confidence in the argument, at some point before you conclude the essay, the reader is likely to make a prediction as to where the argument is going. The reader will begin to sense the final destination and look for landmarks to verify his or her prediction.

You have most likely taken a long trip in a car. If you have never been along the route before, the journey seems to drag on and on. Eventually somebody will ask, "Are we there yet?" This is a question of boredom. You don't want your readers asking themselves, "Are we there yet?" If you have disposed the argument well and the readers can feel the momentum of the argument, they can sense where you are going and know where the destination is. In this case, the readers approach the final paragraphs of the argument with a sense of anticipation, wanting to verify that they know what's around the next turn. And when they arrive, they have the pleasure of knowing that they were right. But this is exactly how you want your readers to feel. You want them to feel that they are right at arriving at the destination that you wanted to lead them to. If you have disposed the argument well, the very disposition will allow your readers the pleasure of saying, "I told you so."

CONCLUSION

Disposition sometimes gets slighted when talking about writing. But in an argument what I hope you have seen is that the disposition is an essential part of the argument; it is part of the argument's persuasive force. By understanding the power of form and the guidelines of disposing an argument, you can meet your readers' expectations for form and reasonableness. If you meet your readers' expectations for form and reasonableness, you will keep your readers reading and will be able to lead them through the entire reasoning process as clearly and as straightforwardly as you can. In addition, you increase the readers' confidence in you as a reasonable, trustworthy person. You increase the reader's confidence in the argument, and you allow the reader the pleasure of beating you to your own conclusion. What could be better than that!

REFERENCE

Burke, K. (1968). *Counter-statement.* Berkeley, CA: University of California Press.

NOTES

NOTES

Chapter

STYLE AND DELIVERY

Letting the Light Shine Through

Deborah Harrison

INTRODUCTION

I remember sitting in my first college English class waiting to get back my first college essay. I had sweated over that essay, spending hours thinking about it and writing it. When I got my essay back I quickly riffled through the pages to look at the grade and the comments on the last page. "Wonderful ideas." That was good. She liked my ideas. "Rather pretentious language." Wait a minute. What did that mean? Hadn't I written exactly how my high school teachers had taught me to write for college? I'd been careful to be formal and I'd thrown in big words and everything. Wasn't that what teachers wanted? That first essay was my initial awakening to the whole idea of style and delivery—and how much they matter in presenting "wonderful ideas."

Can't a brilliant idea speak for itself? Yes and no. What we have to say *and* how we say it matter in persuading an audience. Whenever we write, we enter into a conversation with our readers. It is an odd conversation, to be sure, because both writer and reader are alone; we write in private and readers read in private. The readers can't hear our voice, see our passion for the topic, or ask us questions. As writers we can't force the readers to keep reading. But we can entice readers to continue reading with the freshness of our ideas and the ease of our presentation. We can keep readers from becoming lost or bored. Our task as writers is to think deeply and clearly and to present our ideas in such a way that our readers understand our point of view. That takes good ideas *and* style and delivery.

WHAT IS STYLE?

Style is an elusive term. It has something to do with the idea to be expressed and the individuality of the writer (Harmon & Holman, 2000, p. 500). It encompasses clarity and coherence and conciseness and voice. But it adds up to more than these individual considerations. The essayist E. B. White said, "Style results more from what a person is than from what he knows" (as cited in Murray, 2001, p. 77). And since no two personalities are the same, no two styles are exactly the same. Just as we have our own style of dressing or talking, we have our own style of writing. Our style is made up of the choices we make in presenting our ideas. Do we write longer sentences or shorter sentences, have a chatty style or a more formal approach, use larger words or slang terms? Most of these choices will depend upon the rhetorical situation, upon the subject we are writing about and the audience we are writing to. But even if we change from more formal to informal writing, there is still something that is inherently ours that should shine through our writing.

CLARITY

The first requirement of any writing is that it communicate clearly. In fact, clarity trumps everything. If our readers don't understand what we are saying, then it's a given that they also won't be persuaded to our point of view. Being clear is the ability to express our thoughts in an understandable manner, the ability to reach out to our readers and put us both on the same page.

Clarity is never an easy task; we often don't know exactly what we want to say until after we've written it. Writing forces us to think. The process of writing *is* thinking. That's why clarity usually comes with rewriting. We plop down our ideas on the page, then we go back, once we've understood exactly what we mean to say, and make sure our ideas are clear for our readers.

The ancient rhetoricians had a telling definition of clarity. The Latin terms for clarity (*lucere* "to shine," *perspicere* "to see through,") suggest that clarity once meant language that allowed meaning to "'shine through,' like light through a window" (Crowley & Hawhee, 2004, p. 281). I like that metaphor, the idea of meaning shining through to our readers unimpeded. However, that kind of clarity usually comes at a price—hard work. George M. Trevelyan (1913), a distinguished British historian, backs me up on this point:

> The idea that histories which are delightful to read must be the work of superficial temperaments, and that a crabbed style betokens a deep thinker or conscientious worker, is the reverse of the truth. What is easy to read has been difficult to write. The labor of writing and rewriting, correcting and recorrecting, is the due exacted by every good book from its author. . . . The easily flowing connections of sentence with sentence and paragraph with paragraph has always been won by the sweat of the brow. (p. 34)

Deep or complex ideas need not be expressed in obscure ways. Indeed, they *shouldn't* be.

COHERENCE

"If there is any way for your readers to get lost—they will" (Hairston & Keene, 2003, p. 72). It is true. And it is a good thing to keep in mind because if readers do get lost, it is usually the writer's fault. The burden of communicating falls decisively at the feet of the writer. That is why the ability to connect ideas in a logical manner is so important in the process of persuasion.

A coherent essay is one that simply makes sense; it moves logically and smoothly from idea to idea. In the ideal essay, our "wonderful ideas" fit together like links on a chain. Each link is attached to the link before it and the link after it. There are no holes, no gaps. The readers move smoothly and easily from one point to the next. It is this connection of ideas in our essays that establishes the logic behind our arguments.

One way writers achieve coherence is through the expected three-part structure of an essay (see the discussion of **form** in the previous chapter). Readers expect an introduction, body, and conclusion. Most students, assuming they know this structure, arrive at college fully equipped with the five-paragraph essay. They can pull it out and slap it down in an evening: they write an introduction with a thesis, a body of three paragraphs that supports the thesis, and a conclusion that restates the thesis. However, what most students don't realize is that they are not tied to a five-paragraph essay. There are other ways to work with and look at an essay's structure. The five paragraph essay is a good beginning. But it is not the end. It is a foundation upon which to build.

Keith Hjortshoj (2001) presents another approach to the three-part structure of an essay in his book *The Transition to College Writing*. He compares an essay to a journey we take with our readers. We start at the departure point—making sure our readers know where we are beginning the journey, and why. The body of the essay is the journey itself, carrying the readers smoothly from the point of departure through connected passages (usually more than three paragraphs) until we arrive at a destination. The destination takes us somewhere a little different than where we started—a culminating illumination or insight the readers can now thoroughly embrace because of the journey that led us there (pp. 32–46).

It should be quite clear how the path from the point of departure gets us to the destination. One of the ways writers keep us on the path is by moving smoothly from idea to idea with transition words like *for example, however, first, next,* and *finally.* These words help to guide the reader through the journey. They are the glue that holds ideas together. Notice the difference that exists in the following paragraph from a student essay when the transitions are removed. The first paragraph lacks transitions while the second paragraph retains them.

> Jazz bands began to split into two main categories: black and white. Black bands (bands made up entirely of African-Americans) were known as "big bands." Solos were encouraged among all of the band members, not just the leader of the band. These bands played mostly for the poorer, lower class blacks of the era. These big bands began writing their

own music. The music performed by jazz bands had been made up entirely of arrangements of the day's popular music. Music was written specifically for a band.

Now read the second paragraph with the transitions and note the difference in coherence and flow.

Jazz bands began to split into two main categories: black and white. Black bands (bands made up entirely of African-Americans) were known as "big bands" and *were characterized by a number of things. First,* solos were encouraged among all of the band members, not just the leader of the band. *Second,* these bands played mostly for the poorer, lower class blacks of the era. And *third,* these big bands began writing their own music. *Up until this time,* the music performed by jazz bands had been made up entirely of arrangements of the day's popular music. *It wasn't until this time* that music was written specifically for a band. [Emphasis added.]

The first paragraph seems disjointed. We don't understand how one idea connects to the next. But when transition words are supplied, the ideas link together smoothly, helping readers follow the logic of the ideas.

A colleague of mine compares transition words to markers on a trail. When we hike, we usually watch for markers along the trail to assure us we are on the right path and to encourage us in our journey. The markers let us know how far we have come and how much farther we have to go. They are visual reminders of our progress, and we come to depend on them for a sense of where we are on the path. Transition words in essays are like these markers on a trail: they clearly signal to the reader where we are on the path.

Another way writers keep us on the path is by repeating words that reinforce the relationship of one idea to another. This is accomplished by repeating information that is known before adding new information, thereby creating coherence as well as **cohesion** (see the previous chapter). Notice the links a student writer forges through this type of repetition in the following paragraph:

> The story of how jazz came about begins in New Orleans, Louisiana, around *the turn of the century. During this time,* numerous small bands were commissioned to play for funeral processions as they walked to the *tombs. On the way to the tombs,* the bands would play somber, mournful, music. However, *on the way back,* they would perform more *upbeat* tunes, celebrating the deceased person's life. It was this *upbeat* funeral music that became what we know today as jazz.

It is difficult to get lost when each idea links so clearly to the next. The first words of the second sentence, "During this time," refer to the last words of the first sentence, "the turn of the century." By building on information already presented, we as writers can move the readers along smoothly to a new idea, that "small bands were commissioned to play for funeral processions as they walked to the tombs." Many teachers refer to this as the "flow" of an essay. This flow is what allows us as writers to present the logic of our ideas to our readers in a seamlessly clear manner.

Another important way writers create coherence is by being specific. If we make a general statement, we'd better illustrate it with a specific example (or examples) so we are absolutely positive our readers understand our point. For instance, if we say reading helps to develop imagination, we should back that statement up with scientific research, or personal experience, or examples of when (and how) reading has done this for people. We might cite how the Harry Potter books awakened imagination in children, or we could quote a study with statistics to prove our point. Sweeping generalizations may sound grand, but they do little to clarify and still less to persuade. The more specific we are, the more we can be assured our intended meaning will be understood.

Structure, transitions, repetition, and specifics all help to create coherence that allows us to present our arguments clearly to our readers. Without coherence, our readers get lost and rarely arrive at the same destination as the writer. As William Zinsser (1976) puts it, "If the reader is lost, it is generally because the writer has not been careful enough to keep him on the path" (p. 8). Keeping readers on the right path with clarity and coherence is essential in writing an effective argument.

CONCISENESS

When we write, we want the most amount of power from the least amount of words. This is not to say, however, that we should get rid of words willy-nilly—just unnecessary ones. Some words are part of our style, create coherence, or are needed for the beauty and rhythm of language. But other words simply cloud our intended meaning, causing our readers to fumble about in a fog while they try to figure out what we are trying to say.

Let's look at a possible opening sentence for an essay on *Walden:*

> Henry David Thoreau argues in *Walden* that men spend their lives in "quiet desperation" due to the fact that they are overly preoccupied and busy with lots of things that are of little real value.

When we get rid of all the unnecessary words the sentence has more power because it allows the idea to shine through more clearly.

> Henry David Thoreau argues in *Walden* that men spend their lives in "quiet desperation" because they are preoccupied with things of little value.

We shouldn't use a sentence when a phrase will do; we shouldn't use three words when one word will do. *Due to the fact that* can be replaced with *because; preoccupied* and *busy* mean roughly the same thing, so we lose no meaning when we delete the redundancy. We should get rid of deadwood, those useless, floating pieces of language that clog up our sentences and add no meaning: *really, very, rather, so, quite.*

Conciseness in language eliminates the fog and gives our ideas more power. As the stylist William Strunk says, "Vigorous writing is concise. A sentence should contain no unnecessary words, a paragraph no unnecessary sentences, for the same reason that a drawing should have no unnecessary lines and a machine no unnecessary parts" (1979, p. 23).

VOICE

Voice is probably the first thing I look for in deciding whether I will continue to read something or not. What do I mean by voice? I mean that you, your personality, or how you want readers to perceive you comes off the page, that I can hear you speaking in your own matchless way, that I can feel you genuinely wish to engage me as your reader. It means there is a quality and genuineness to the writing that sets you apart from all other writers. Voice is like putting your thumbprint on anything you write. If you were to enter my house and steal my television, but you left your thumbprint on my wall, I could track you down and find you (and recover my television) because no one in the world has your exact thumbprint. We should have our thumbprint on everything we write. We shouldn't put aside who we are when we pick up a pen to write. Even if we are writing formal essays we can still maintain our voice, though it will be more subdued.

The first essay I wrote for my first college class lacked voice. That's what my professor meant when she said, "Rather pretentious language." My high school teachers had taught me to write so formally in preparation for college that I had all but obliterated my own voice. It took me many years to find it again. When I teach the concept of voice to my students, I encourage them to discover their own voices if they have lost them (or never found them). I assure them that their voice matters, and it can make a difference in the world. This concept seems to lift a burden from their shoulders. It is as if I have released them from a self-imposed prison: "I matter. My voice matters." Indeed it does.

Writing that has voice is far more engaging than writing that lacks it. Consider the following response on the topic "Education":

> Education is of paramount importance in today's society. Young people today simply can't make it without a college education. A college education teaches young adults how to think, manage time, and be well rounded individuals. College students shouldn't take their education for granted but should work hard so they can succeed in today's world.

This response could have been written by any number of people. It does not have the voice of an individual shining through it, and therefore it fails to engage us as readers. Donald Murray (2001) has identified several other reasons that cause writing to lack voice: no intellectual challenge, no emotional challenge, no flow of energy that propels the readers forward (pp. 69–70). The response on education suffers from all of these maladies. Besides not having an individual personality coming through the writing, the paragraph lacks intellectual depth and emotional appeal. The author has said nothing new or interesting about education and so fails to engage the reader, one of the functions of voice. The writing makes sense, it flows, but it is boring—thus it doesn't propel us forward with anticipation for the next idea.

If voice makes such a difference in writing, how might we go about finding our voice? By being willing to be ourselves, by being willing to be honest, vulnerable, passionate. Notice the delightful yet quite diverse voices that emerge in the following samples.

> The primary difference between men and women is that women can see extremely small quantities of dirt. Not when they're babies, of course. Babies of both sexes have a very low awareness of dirt, other than to think it tastes better than food. (Barry, 1988, p. 219)

> On a morning in May 1804, there arrived at the White House . . . a visitor from abroad: an aristocratic young German, age thirty-four, a bachelor, occupation scientist and explorer. And like Halley's comet or the white whale or other such natural phenomena dear to the nineteenth century, he would be remembered by all who saw him for the rest of their days. (McCullough, 1992, p. 3)

> My husband and I got married at eight in the morning. It was winter, freezing, the trees encased in ice and a few lone blackbirds balancing on telephone wires. We were in our early 30s, considered ourselves hip and cynical, the types who decried the institution of marriage even as we sought its status. (Slater, 2006, p. 32)

All of these samples are well written and effective. Barry's voice is informal and humorous. McCollough's voice is more formal, with longer sentences and bigger words, yet there is a pleasure in the refined tone. Slater's voice is engaging—promising well thought out insights and stark honesty. Who these authors are shines through their writing and sets their writing apart as their own. It is unlikely that anyone would mistake Barry's writing for McCullough's. It should be just as unlikely that anyone would mistake our writing for another's.

Our voice begins to come off the page with the first words we write. The title is usually a good indication of what we can expect from an essay. A good title should tantalize us to want to read more. Walker Percy puts it well: "A good title should be like a metaphor: It should intrigue without being too baffling or too obvious" (as cited in Trimble, 2000, p. 180). For example, a humanities class was assigned to write an essay arguing whether the cathedrals in the Middle Ages should have been humbly built and adorned or richly built and adorned (as they were). One student entitled her essay, "Forget the Poor— I Want a Gold Door." Another entitled it "Cathedrals in the Middle Ages." Which essay would you want to read first? As Geoffrey Parsons so clearly explains, "I place great emphasis on a title and a first sentence. You must think of your potential reader as a shy and reclusive trout. . . . Your task, is to cast a fly so vivid and appealing that forgetting all else he will leap at your bait" (as cited in Trimble, 2000, p. 180). Voice helps this leap to occur.

Another consideration in creating voice is what person to write in. Which person we choose, either first, second, or third person, affects the distance we create between ourselves and our readers. Depending on what our relationship is to our subject or our audience, we might want to lessen or widen the distance from our readers. For instance, the choice to write in first person (I, we) creates less distance between the writer and reader. It is less formal and more conversational. Using *we* distinctly lessens the distance because now the readers are included and feel a part of what is being said. However, while the first person lessens distance, it can sometimes lessen authority since it is less formal. Second person speaking (you) can be a tricky choice. If done well, the use of *you* can be seen as informal and chatty—and bring the audience closer. Done poorly, it can take on an authoritative, even superior, tone that can create distance since it can come across like a lecture—and few people enjoy being lectured. The third person choice (he, she, they, one) pushes the subject to the forefront, since references to the writer or reader disappear. This choice is more formal and creates the most distance between the writer and reader, but it can also establish more authority as the facts are allowed to speak for themselves.

Notice the change in tone and distance that occurs when the following narrative is changed from the first person to the third person.

> As I remember it, my story always starts out like a fairy tale. . . . Once upon a time in Paris, between two world wars, there lived a happy little boy. I was that little boy. (Lusseyran, 1987, p. 5)

> As he remembers it, his story always starts out like a fairy tale. . . . Once upon a time in Paris, between two world wars, there lived a happy little boy. He was that little boy.

In this case, there is far more power in the first example than in the second. The first example engages us in a real story; the second distances us from it as we stand back to observe it.

Choice of tense also affects voice and distance. The present tense has more immediacy than the past tense, since it gives readers a sense of participating in events as they are unfolding. The past tense can make readers feel that they are only standing back and observing events that have already happened. Notice the difference that tense makes in the following two sentences:

> The boy reaches into his pocket and takes out a coin.

> The boy reached into his pocket and took out a coin.

In the first sentence we feel that we are there, watching the boy pull out the coin. In the second sentence, we feel as if it has already happened and we are just standing back observing what has occurred.

Word choice and levels of formality can also affect the sense of voice. It is fine to use a big word if the big word is the right word. However, throwing around big words just to sound smart doesn't usually improve a writer's credibility. The use of the word *paramount* in the paragraph on "Education" sounds educated but lacks power since we're not even sure the writer knows what *paramount* means. But using a big word that is the right word is also the right choice. Mark Twain is quoted as saying, "The difference between the right word and the almost right word is like the difference between lightning and the lightning bug" (as cited in Marlowe, 2001). We want the right word to carry our intended meaning to our audience. If we change our words, we also change how our audience interprets our meaning. For instance, if we want to say that something needs to be done, it matters whether we choose to use the word *imperative, necessary* or *helpful* to convey that message. The different word choices convey a different sense of urgency.

We also need to pay attention to the level of formality in our writing. How much formality do we need to reel in our audience and have them accept our points? There is danger in writing too formally (we bore or lose our readers) or too informally (we could offend or lose credibility). Usually choosing the middle ground, what Wilma and David Ebbitt call the General English style, is the best choice, leaning a little to one side or the other as the topic or audience demands (1990, xiv–xv). In the General English style we avoid the dangers of falling into clichés (dark as night), slang terms (cool, hot), colloquialisms (Oh, my gosh), or sounding so formal that we could be stuffed and hung up to dry (It behooves me to remind you that your rent is inordinately past due).

Writing that has voice is more engaging and enhances meaning. The early Greek rhetoricians must have understood this concept, since originally in Greek the word *logos* meant "voice" or "speech." It was only later that logos also came to be associated with reason (Crowley & Hawhee, 2004, p. 20). Thus, voice and reason work hand in hand. Voice adds magic to our ideas: "The magic of writing is that the voice arises from the spaces between the words as much as from the words themselves, carrying meaning to the reader" (Murray, 2001, p. 70). This magic helps to establish our credibility with our readers and can affect the emotional attachment that our readers have to our ideas. These issues are crucial in persuading an audience.

DELIVERY, DELIVERY, DELIVERY

There was an ancient orator who, when asked what was the most important part of effective rhetoric, said, "Delivery, delivery, delivery" (as cited in Lunsford, Ruszkiewicz & Walters, 2001, p. 292). Of course, he was referring to oral presentation, to body language and voice inflection. But the same could be said today about written communication. It's important to pay attention to the details of delivery, our punctuation, usage, and layout, so that our ideas can be more easily understood and accepted.

Consider for a moment the following letter that was a mass mailing to potential clients. The real estate agent is hoping to drum up business by persuading his audience that he is qualified to handle their real estate needs.

Dear Homeowner,

I would like to introduce myself. My name is_____. And I am a new real estate agent in the _____ area.. The past seven years I have been working as a Golf Professional. As a golf professional and working with a diverse group of clientele. I gained an invaluable experience in customer relations.

This is an exciting step for me and I would be thrilled to have you apart of it! If you have been thinking about buying or selling-residential or commercial; or if you know of anyone who is thinking of buying or selling a home. Give me a call, and let me help you with all of your real estate necessities.

It is possible that this individual *is* quite qualified to handle the real estate needs of his clientele—but his credibility is definitely compromised when he doesn't pay closer attention to the delivery of his letter. There are minor errors (capitalizing Golf Professional and including two periods) and there are major errors in sentence structure and punctuation. For instance, there are sentence fragments that impede understanding and cause the reader to have to reread for meaning: "As a golf professional and working with a diverse group of clientele." Where does this idea belong? With the sentence before it or the sentence after? And glaring punctuation errors also impede understanding: "If you have been thinking about buying or selling-residential or commercial; or if you know of anyone who is thinking of buying or selling a home" (the semicolon should actually be another dash—but it's a sentence fragment nonetheless). Even though the agent is obviously excited about his new career and is direct in his approach, because he hasn't taken the time to carefully craft and proofread the letter, many potential clients may arrive at the same conclusion: "If he doesn't take the time to attend to the details of a simple letter, how can I be sure I can trust him to attend to the details of my real estate transactions?" In other words, his lack of attention to delivery hurts his credibility and lessens his ability to persuade his audience. Just this morning a friend of mine called and mentioned that she had considered joining a particular online dating service but had decided against it when she noticed several obvious errors in spelling and punctuation. Does delivery matter in convincing an audience? It most definitely does.

Punctuation

Punctuation choices can affect our ability to persuade the reader. As with the letter from the real estate agent, our attention to the details of our written communication can affect both the logic of our ideas and the credibility of our ideas.

In matters of punctuation we have some advantages over our ancient counterparts in Greece and Rome. They had no punctuation marks. And what is even harder to imagine, all written works were done in *scriptio continua*, meaning that there weren't even spaces between the words. In classical times all writing was meant to be read out loud, whether in private or public, so learning how to read the words, where to put the appropriate pauses and emphasis, was an art that took practice. The first punctuation marks were created to help actors in Greek dramas know where to breathe. Later they were used by teachers to help their students learn how to read a text out loud. So the first punctuation marks were rhetorical and used to enhance oral interpretation.

When reading became a silent, private affair during the Middle Ages, punctuation marks were needed to guide the reader along. Charlemagne recognized that something needed to be done about the mess writing was in, so in A.D. 781 he asked his minister of education, Alcuin of York, to set things right. Alcuin set up a school that the monks attended, and by the ninth century we had a standardized writing style that included lower case letters, arrangement into sentences and paragraphs, and some punctuation marks (complete translation.com, 2005). However, it wasn't until the invention of the printing press in 1436 that we finally started to solidify the marks of punctuation to help in silent reading. For nearly two hundred years printers tinkered with punctuation marks until by the 1700s the system we know today was generally in place.

Today, since most reading is done silently and alone, punctuation has become the subtle means by which we as authors can extend meaning to our readers. Since readers don't have the luxury of our facial gestures or tone, our punctuation must take up that slack. It is for this reason that I see punctuation as an art—not just as a collection of rules. Granted, there are rules that we must follow, but I like to think of punctuation as rules that help us know how to create tone and enhance meaning. Even the rules give us choices. In this light, punctuation becomes as much of an art form as painting or drawing. In these art forms, the choice to use a single line here or there can make considerable difference in how an art work is viewed or the feeling surrounding the work. For instance, a diagonal line in a drawing creates tension as the viewer waits for the line to right itself or fall. So it is with punctuation: a single choice of which punctuation mark to use in a given place can change the tone of the sentence or the actual meaning of the sentence. Take the following sentence, a popular example that has been used by teachers for years to demonstrate the value of punctuation:

A woman, without her man, is nothing.

A woman: without her, man is nothing.

In the first sentence a woman can't be without her man, but in the second, the man can't be without the woman. Quite a difference in meaning to convey with only punctuation marks! And consider the difference punctuation choice makes in the following example:

I must see him at once—at once, not later.

I must see him at once . . . at once, not later.

In the first sentence the dash gives boldness to the sentence; we can almost hear the speaker pounding on the desk. In the second sentence the ellipsis creates mystery, a pause for consideration.

Sometimes a punctuation mark may convey a special kind of meaning that cannot be achieved efficiently any other way. Lynne Truss (2003) gives an excellent example of the difference in meaning that punctuation choices can make in her book *Eats, Shoots, & Leaves.*

See how the sense changes with the punctuation in this example:

Tom locked himself in the shed. England lost to Argentina.

These two statements as they stand, could be quite unrelated. They merely tell you two things have happened, in the past tense.

Tom locked himself in the shed; England lost to Argentina.

We can infer from the semicolon that these events occurred at the same time, although it is possible that Tom locked himself in the shed because he couldn't bear to watch the match and therefore still doesn't know the outcome. . . .

Tom locked himself in the shed: England lost to Argentina.

> All is now clear. Tom locked himself in the shed *because* England lost to Argentina. And who can blame him, that's what I say. (pp. 129–130)

The sentences remained the same. All that changed was the punctuation. But the punctuation changed the meaning and the tone. Only a semicolon can tell a reader that these two sentences are closely related in the writer's mind. Only a colon can inform the reader that what follows is a direct result of what came before. These are subtle nuances that punctuation can effectively convey.

It's important for us to know the rules—the accepted conventions—but it's also important for us to know when it is appropriate to bend those rules for our rhetorical purposes. The stylist Joseph Williams (2000) refers to this as learning to observe rules thoughtfully (pp. 20–21). I had experience with this whole idea of learning to observe rules thoughtfully when I was a teenager growing up in southern California. I had asked my dad, an avid tennis player, to teach me how to play tennis. The first thing he did was put the tennis racket in my hand and say, "This racket is an extension of your arm. You no longer have a wrist. If a ball comes at you low, don't break your wrist to hit it back, but bend down from your knees to meet it so that you can hit it back without bending your wrist." I believed him. I learned my backhand and forehand and was coming along nicely—until we were practicing one hot Saturday afternoon.

The heat was taking its toll and sweat was trickling down the side of my face. I began to get tired of bending down to meet all those low balls. Then I noticed that my dad wasn't doing what he had told me to do. When I hit a ball low over the net, he bent his wrist and just whisked it back at me—without bending down to meet it. *Well,* I thought to myself, *I'm hot, I'm tired, I'm going to bend my wrist, too.* So I did. For the next ball that came to me. But it didn't go over the net. It just bounced back miserably and landed at my feet. Not to be discouraged, I tried it again when a ball came over low—with the same results. My dad glared at me over the net. He hit the next ball very hard and very low, and when I failed to return that ball as well (admittedly, I was a slow learner), he motioned to me to meet him at the net and he came striding forward to deliver his lecture. It was a simple one. "You can't break the rules until you know the rules. Now go back and hit the ball the way I taught you!" He had been playing tennis for forty years by that time and he understood perfectly what it took to get the ball back over the net. I, on the other hand, was a beginner, and I didn't yet know enough to break the rules and still have them work for me.

The same is true of the conventions of English—particularly punctuation rules. We need to know the rules so well that we understand when it is appropriate, for our purposes, to break those rules. For instance, many teachers preach about the sins of sentence fragments and tell their students to avoid fragments at all costs. However, a sentence fragment can actually carry great power—if it is used appropriately. The real estate agent used a sentence fragment that didn't carry power: "As a golf professional working with a diverse group of clientele." This is because the fragment caused confusion, most likely because the author didn't realize he was using a fragment. I used a fragment in telling the tennis story: "So I did. *For the next ball that came to me.*" I did it on purpose. I did it because I felt the fragment would create more emphasis and thus more power. The truth is that most great writers use fragments for effect. The difference is that these writers know they are using a fragment and they know what effect they want to create with that fragment. They also know when the formality of the subject matter or the audience would render a fragment inappropriate. They have learned to "observe rules thoughtfully."

It matters that we understand the rules of punctuation and that we use them with judgment and good taste. Using punctuation well helps to establish credibility with our readers. Sometimes it is quite clear what punctuation marks should be used—an obvious rule that dictates what is right or wrong. At other times we may have many choices that are acceptable, each with their accompanying tone and subtle nuance of meaning. In these instances, we'll need to rely on our common sense for the best choice. In the end, we simply want our readers to understand our intended message. Effective punctuation helps us achieve this goal.

USAGE AND LAYOUT

As with any written communication, it's important to always keep in mind the audience we are addressing and the purpose for which we are addressing them. In the back of our minds we should keep the constant nagging thought that ultimately we are writing to persuade someone of something. How best to do that? Style matters, as we have already discussed, as do punctuation choices. But we should keep in mind a few other considerations of delivery: usage and layout.

Usage has to do with how we actually use the language, our choice of appropriate words. Some people think of it as linguistic etiquette. Just as we probably wouldn't choose to show up in sweats and an old T-shirt for a formal dinner to meet our future in-laws, we shouldn't choose language that will offend or distance our audience from us. We should always write to be inclusive of gender, race, or ethnic groups.

Before the Feminist Movement of the '60s and '70s, the so-called generic "he" was used to refer to both male and female. Since that time, however, the generic "he" has fallen out of grace, and all careful writers avoid its use in favor of more inclusive terms. Probably the easiest way to include everyone is to use the plural—either "they" or "we." But if writers choose to use the singular, they must also be careful to include both "he and she" in all their writing. The following sentence, for example, does not use inclusive language:

A good writer knows that *he* should strive for clarity.

This sentence can easily be rewritten to include everyone without sacrificing style or meaning:

Good writers know that they should strive for clarity.

We know that writers should strive for clarity.

A good writer knows that he or she should strive for clarity.

Why does including everyone matter? Some readers might become offended or be so caught up in how we are saying things that they miss what we are trying to say—and therefore are never persuaded to our point of view. An example. I was reading through an article in a magazine that was encouraging me, as a parent, to help increase my child's vocabulary by entering my child in a vocabulary contest that offered scholarships to college.

> A strong vocabulary helps kids score higher on SATs, gives them an advantage on college admissions and can even help them win thousands of dollars in college scholarships. So what are you waiting for? Sign your child up . . . and get *him* started. ("Give Your Child the Verbal Edge," 2005, p. 12) [Emphasis added.]

Wait, wait, wait. *Him?* Only boys? Are girls excluded? Not as bright? Is the article suggesting that my daughters aren't as intelligent or as capable as my sons? That girls aren't as good as boys? That as a female I'm inferior? As you can see, I've gotten so caught up in a word choice that I've missed the main point, which is that my children could improve their vocabulary and win scholarships. It is possible to become so caught up in word choices that the intended audience misses the point altogether. We want to avoid that by choosing our words carefully. We should always try to be inclusive in our language.

Similarly, we should be careful to avoid any unnecessary references to race or ethnic groups. If these points of information are not relevant to our argument then we should leave the information out of our remarks. If race or ethnic group is pivotal to our argument then we need to be careful to refer to the race or ethnic group in the manner they prefer (is *black* more appropriate in this instance or *African American?*) and we need to be sure our handling of the information is fair and doesn't fall into stereotypes. For instance, it would be unfair (and untrue) to suggest that all Arabs are terrorists. Our goal is to draw in our audience so they will be persuaded by our penetrating ideas and our obvious good sense; we do not wish to exclude or offend our audience, distancing them from us and our ideas.

Another consideration of delivery is to take care with the visual **layout** of a written argument. A good page layout is a type of persuasion in and of itself. It persuades us initially that we want to read the page. It shows that the writer cares enough about what he or she is writing to consider all aspects of the presentation of the idea. Is the page visually appealing and does the white space invite reading? If we use visuals, are they appropriately placed within the text? Are the paragraphs so long they are daunting? Is the font distracting? While we usually stay with Times Roman font for all academic papers, it is possible to use *italic* typeface for emphasis within the text. Italics calls attention to the words in a refined manner (Do it *now*). In an academic paper, using all capitals for emphasis (DO IT NOW) is overkill, as is bolded (Do it **now**) and overuse of exclamation points (Do it now!!!). In addition, if a paper is longer it is often helpful for readers to have headings and subheadings to "chunk" information together for easier digestion, as has been done in this chapter with the major heading "What is Style?" and the subheadings "Clarity," "Coherence," "Conciseness," and "Voice." Headings can make it easier to identify the main points and to more clearly understand how they fit together.

CONCLUSION

When I wrote my first college essay, so many years ago, I had not understood the value of style and delivery in presenting my "wonderful ideas." I had not understood how much style and delivery matter in creating credibility, meaning, and emotion. I understand their value now, and work hard to present ideas clearly and coherently to my readers. As writers we should try to make the journey for our readers a pleasurable one, where they don't get lost in the fog, or bored, or distanced from our ideas. We should strive for the clarity the Greeks alluded to, one that allows meaning to shine through unimpeded to the readers.

REFERENCES

Barry, D. (1988). Batting clean-up and striking out. In *Dave Barry's greatest hits*, (p. 219). New York: Crown.

Complete translation. (n.d.). *A history of punctuation.* Retrieved March 18, 2005, from http://www.completetranslation. com/punctuation.htm

Crowley, S. & Hawhee, D. (2004). *Ancient rhetorics for contemporary students* (3rd ed.). New York: Pearson Longman.

Ebbitt, W. R. & Ebbitt, D. (1990). *Index to English* (8th ed.) New York: Oxford University Press.

Give your child the verbal edge—and a scholarship. (2005, September). *Reader's Digest*, 12.

Hairston, M. & Keene, M. (2003). *Successful writing* (5th ed.). New York: W. W. Norton.

Harmon, W. &. Holman, C. H. (2000). *A handbook to literature.* (8th ed.). Upper Saddle River, NJ: Prentice Hall.

Hjortshoj, K. (2001). Footstools and furniture. In *The transition to college writing.* (pp. 32–46). Boston, MA: Bedford/St. Martin's.

Lusseyran, J. (1987). *And there was light.* New York: Parabola.

Lunsford, A. & Ruszkiewicz, J. (2001). *Everything's an argument.* Boston: Bedford/St. Martin's.

Marlowe, M. E. (Ed.). (2001). *The importance of words.* Retrieved March 24, 2006, from http:www.bible-researcher.com/language-quotes.html

McCullough, D. (1992). Journey to the top of the world. In *Brave companions.* (pp. 3–19). New York: Touchstone.

Murray, D. M. (2001). *The craft of revision* (4th ed.). Boston, MA: Thomson Heinle.

Slater, L. (2006, February) True love. *National Geographic*, 32–49.

Strunk, W. M. (with White, E. B.). (1979). *Elements of style* (3rd ed.) New York: Macmillan Publishing.

Trevelyan, G. M. (1913). *Clio, a muse and other essays literary and pedestrian.* London: Longman.

Trimble, J. R. (2000). *Writing with style* (2nd ed.). Upper Saddle River, NJ: Prentice-Hall.

Truss, L. (2003). *Eats, shoots, & leaves.* New York: Gotham Books.

Williams, J. M. (2000). *Style.* (6th ed.). New York: Longman.

Zinsser, W. (1976). *On writing well.* New York: Harper & Row.

NOTES